Cabins, Cottages & Mansions

Homes of the Presidents of the United States

by
Nancy D. Myers Benbow
and
Christopher H. Benbow

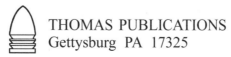

THOMAS PUBLICATIONS
Gettysburg PA 17325

For Our Families,
Whose Aid and Encouragement
Helped to Make This Book Possible
And
For All Who Love American History.

Table of Contents

FOREWORD 5

GEORGE WASHINGTON 8
    George Washington Birthplace National Monument
    Mount Vernon
    Deshler-Morris House

JOHN ADAMS & JOHN QUINCY ADAMS 10
    Adams National Historical Park (Adams Birthplaces)
    Adams National Histoic Site (The Old House)

THOMAS JEFFERSON 12
    Tuckahoe Plantation
    Monticello
    Thomas Jefferson's Poplar Forest

JAMES MADISON 14
    Montpelier

JAMES MONROE 15
    Ash Lawn-Highland
    Oak Hill Farm

ANDREW JACKSON 16
    Museum of the Waxhaws & Andrew Jackson Memorial
    The Hermitage

MARTIN VAN BUREN 17
    Martin Van Buren National Historic Site
        Lindenwald

WILLIAM HENRY HARRISON 18
    Berkeley Plantation
    Grouseland

JOHN TYLER 19
    Sherwood Forest Plantation

JAMES KNOX POLK 20
    James K. Polk State Historic Site
    James K. Polk Ancestral Home

ZACHARY TAYLOR 21
    Springfield

MILLARD FILLMORE 22
    Millard Fillmore Birthplace
    Millard Fillmore House Museum

FRANKLIN PIERCE 23
    Franklin Pierce Homestead
    Pierce Manse

JAMES BUCHANAN 25
    Buchanan's Log Cabin Birthplace
    Buchanan's Birthplace State Historical Park
    Wheatland

ABRAHAM LINCOLN 26
    Abraham Lincoln Birthplace National Historic Site
    Lincoln's Boyhood Home
    Lincoln Boyhood National Memorial
    Lincoln State Park
    Lincoln's New Salem State Historic Site
    Lincoln Home National Historic Site
    Anderson Cottage

ANDREW JOHNSON 30
    Andrew Johnson Birthplace
    Andrew Johnson National Historic Site

ULYSSES SIMPSON GRANT 31
    Grant Birthplace State Historic Site
    Grant Boyhood Home
    Ulysses S. Grant National Historic Site (White Haven)
    Grant's Farm (Hardscrapple)
    U.S. Grant Home State Historical Site
    Grant Cottage State Historic Site

RUTHERFORD BIRCHARD HAYES 34
    Rutherford B. Hayes Presidential Center (Spiegel Grove)

JAMES ABRAM GARFIELD 35
    James A. Garfield National Historic Site (Lawnfield)

CHESTER ALAN ARTHUR 36
    Chester A. Arthur Historic Site

GROVER CLEVELAND 37
    Grover Cleveland Birthplace State Historic Site

BENJAMIN HARRISON 39
    President Benjamin Harrison Home

WILLIAM McKINLEY 40
    The Saxon McKinley House

THEODORE ROOSEVELT 42
    Theodore Roosevelt Birthplace National Historic Site
    Maltese Cross Cabin
    Sagamore Hill National Historic Site
    Pine Knot

WILLIAM HOWARD TAFT 45
    William Howard Taft National Historic Site

WOODROW WILSON 46
    Woodrow Wilson Birthplace
    Woodrow Wilson Boyhood Home – GA
    Woodrow Wilson Boyhood Home – SC
    Woodrow Wilson House

WARREN GAMALIEL HARDING 48
    Warren G. Harding Home

CALVIN COOLIDGE 49
    The Plymouth Notch Historic District
    The Beeches

HERBERT HOOVER 51
    Herbert Hoover National Historic Site
    The Hoover-Minthorn House
    Lou Henry Hoover House

FRANKLIN DELANO ROOSEVELT 53
    Home of Franklin D. Roosevelt
    Roosevelt Campobello International Park
    Little White House and Museum

HARRY S TRUMAN 55
    Harry S Truman Birthplace State Historic Site
    The Truman Farm House
    Harry S Truman National Historic Site
    The Little White House and Museum

DWIGHT DAVID EISENHOWER 58
    Eisenhower Birthplace State Historic Site
    Eisenhower Center
    Eisenhower National Historic Site

JOHN FITZGERALD KENNEDY 60
    John Fitzgerald Kennedy National Historic Site

LYNDON BAINES JOHNSON 61
    Lyndon B. Johnson State Historic Site
    Lyndon B. Johnson National Historical Park

RICHARD MILHOUS NIXON 62
    The Richard Nixon Library & Birthplace

GERALD RUDOLPH FORD 63
    Gerald R. Ford Birthsite Park

JAMES EARL CARTER 64
    Jimmy Carter National Historic Site

RONALD WILSON REAGAN 65
    Ronald Reagan Birthplace
    Ronald Reagan Boyhood Home
    The California Governor's Mansion

GEORGE HERBERT WALKER BUSH 67
    George Bush Birthplace
    Bush Summer Home/Summer White House
    Vice President's Residence

WILLIAM JEFFERSON CLINTON 70
    The Arkansas Governor's Mansion
    The Clinton Center

GEORGE WALKER BUSH 72

THE WHITE HOUSE 73

BEFORE THEY BECAME PRESIDENT 77

BIBLIOGRAPHY 79

Foreword to 3rd Edition of

Cabins, Cottages and Mansions: Homes of the Presidents of the United States

Our homes shape us; whether we were born in a cottage, or a mansion, or a city apartment, the personality of our childhood home influences our lives. As adults, we choose our homes more or less consciously, to reflect who we are (or who we want to be). In America, there is an amazing variety of house types, and yet, with allowance for regional and ethnic preferences as well as historical period, there is also a consistency in the American home. By the mid-19th century in America, there was a very clear sense of what "home" should be. Immigrant groups, whatever customs they retained, seem to have adopted the American sense of "home" quickly. America's chief peculiarity as a nation is its paradoxical desire for individuality and personal expression, combined with an equally intense desire for commonality and shared experience. By the middle of the 20th century, when I was born, the American home had become a monolithic reality, and yet within that homogeneity there was, and remains, a complexity that echoes the complexity of the American personality.

There are two reasons why I am glad to have the chance to write this foreword to Chris and Nancy Benbow's book about the cottages, cabins and mansions that shaped the men who have held this nation's highest office. First, as a museum curator and caretaker of a remarkable 19th-century urban house, I understand the great appeal that historic houses have. Second, as a great-great grandson of Ulysses S. and Julia D. Grant, I appreciate the important role that houses can play in a person's life, and how much we can learn about famous people from their homes.

Since my childhood I have loved old houses, and their ability to transport me to different times. As an adult I have spent my career studying the rich potential that houses have to illuminate the characters of the people who build them, furnish them, and grow up in them. A house that survives many generations in one family (like Teddy and Eddy Roosevelt's Sagamore Hill) becomes a material archive of that family's history. A restored historic house, such as Mount Vernon or Monticello, although it might lack the layered authenticity of an unbroken chain of ownership, can also provide visitors with a deeper understanding of the world in which it was inhabited, providing that the right research has been done. These last two examples, because of the fame and importance of their presidential owners, have been carefully preserved and dramatically research and furnished. But even a house where only the building itself survives, bereft of family furnishings or documents, can, all by itself, tell you a great deal about the family who lived there. The building itself — the way it is built, its style, its setting, the shape of its rooms — all had an influence on the people who lived (and died) there.

The Ballantine House in Newark, New Jersey, is not a presidential house, but it can serve as an example of how even empty houses can bring the past to life. It was acquired by The Newark Museum as an office building in 1937, and not valued as a

historic building until the Bicentennial in 1976 inspired the first restoration project. It was an empty house, rich in architectural detail, but devoid of family documents. Over the years the museum has accumulated some wonderful documents relating to the house, enabling us to redecorate and refurnish some of the rooms as they might have been when the Ballantine family lived there. Some of the original furnishings have come back to the museum from the Ballantine family, but most are taken from the museum's own huge collection of decorative arts. Nonetheless, while we have not been able to exactly recreate the house in which John and Jeannette Ballantine raised their children and grandchildren, we have, through careful research and interpretation, been able to give our visitors a vivid experience that helps them understand what life in Newark would have been like over a century ago.

In terms of my presidential ancestor, it is through my love of houses that I have come to know my namesake Ulysses, and my mother's namesake, Julia. Being a house-nut by the age of twelve, it was always through houses that I saw my own family — the house I grew up in; my grandparents' houses, the houses of relatives near and far. All of those houses were inextricable from my understanding of my large, scattered family. Eventually, as I delved back further in my family history, I began to find pictures of houses that were in my family's past. Thus I happened on the hotel cottage at Mt. McGregor, New York, where my namesake died, and began my quest to understand Ulysses and Julia through their houses. Quite frankly, I have never liked the history of way and politics as much as the history of decorating and furnishing. That is why I am a decorative arts curator. That is also why I read Julia Grant's memoirs twice before I picked up the General's far more famous memoirs. Ulysses talked about the War. Julia talked about her curtains and her carpeting, her silver and her Dresden china. She talked about home.

Ulysses and Julia Grant's entire life can be summarized by the houses they occupied; indeed their lives, from their respective births in the 1820s to the General's death in 1885 at Mt. McGregor, are emblematic of the life of the entire nation in the same period. The incredible range of houses that Ulysses and Julia and their children lived in is astonishing – log cabin, city townhouse, suburban villa, the White House. Sadly, many of these historic homes have not survived, and exist today only as images preserved in engravings, drawings, or photographs. Julia was born in a small, vernacular plantation house on the frontier — and it is important to remember that it was frontier when her parents moved there. Ulysses was born in a cottage in rural Ohio, as sure a sign of his modest beginnings as Lincoln's own mythical log cabin was. The Dent family house, White Haven, near St. Louis, was eventually left to Ulysses by Julia's father, Frederick Dent. Ulysses' childhood home in Georgetown, Ohio, survives in private hands. Neither of these houses is furnished as they would have been originally, but both offer the visitor valuable insight into the settings that shaped this couple as children and as a married couple. Interestingly, the Grants and the Dents were probably not that far apart financially in the 1830s, although the spartan, abolitionist Jesse Grant raised his children in a very different world from the indulgent, slave-owning, self-styled planter Colonel Dent. White Haven was in fact Ulysses and Julia's only permanent home until Ulysses left the Army in the 1850s, and built Hardscrabble. This is perhaps the Grants' best known home, because of the Busch family's careful preservation of it, and due to its display at the 1904 Louisiana Purchase Exposition in St. Louis. It was also the house Julia liked least — because it was a "guy" house — all logs and rough wilderness, while she yearned for gentility and suburban comfort. The neat little house that they rented in Galena, Illinois, after Ulysses gave up farming and went into clerking for one of his father's branch leather shops, gives the lie to the myth that Grant was a failure. It is a pleasant, cozy and (for a time) spacious enough middle-class house. If it speaks of anything, it speaks of a stable, unremarkable shopkeeper's life — a dull life that drove Grant to distraction and probably back into the army at the outbreak of the Civil War. (And a good thing, too, I might add.)

Their next house in Galena, given to them fully furnished upon their triumphant return in 1865, seems as if it should have been the answer to all of Julia's dreams. It is an extremely rare house, from a curator's perspective, in that it retains its original furnishings, and represents the archetypal suburban middle-class house of the period. That too, is this house's problem — it is a model house, not Julia's house. It does not really represent Julia's taste, because it was fully furnished when they got it. And the real reason it is so perfectly preserved is that, as soon as Julia and Ulysses had tasted fame and fortune in the East, that is where they went. Like so many Americans, they were drawn to the capitals of politics and finance: Washington and New York. Sadly, their big, expensive house in Georgetown, near Washington, is long gone, but we know from a few surviving furnishings that Julia's taste expanded with her husband's celebrity and pocketbook. I cannot imagine that Ulysses himself really cared if he owned any silver from Tiffany & Co., or that he cooked up the idea of ordering a 365-piece dinner service with his monogram on it from China. But I know Julia must have loved this shopping, and all of it went into the Georgetown house in 1868 — and then into what was undoubtedly Julia's favorite house of all in 1869, the White House.

It has been said that the White House was loved by Julia Grant more than by any other first lady. She certainly enjoyed her eight years there, and regretted leaving it for the rest of her life. The saddest loss, to me as a curator and a descendant, was the house that embodied the Grants' brief but dazzling post-Presidency glory — the wide brownstone mansion at 3 East 66th Street — one house in from the fabled Fifth Avenue. Only black and white engravings and photographs remain to suggest the opulence of this high-Victorian townhouse, and few of the furnishings have survived, victims of changing taste and times. Even though the Grants only lived in the house as a couple for five years, it was, next to the White House, the place that most characterized how their lives had evolved. After the General's bankruptcy, my great-grandparents, Frederick and Ida Grant, moved from Morristown, New Jersey, into the 66th Street house, and thus my grandfather, Ulysses S. Grant III, spent his early years there.

Julia sold that house and moved to Washington in the 1890s. The 66th Street house was torn down in 1926 and replaced by a small apartment building. So while only a bronze plaque marks the location of the house where Ulysses and Julia lived their last years together, the hotel cottage outside of Saratoga, New York, where Ulysses lived for only a month, remains eerily frozen in time to the moment on July 23, 1885, when he gave up his battle against cancer. While the Mt. McGregor cottage is a wonderful place to visit, it is important as a house only because it demonstrates how determined Ulysses was to finish his memoirs, and thus leave his widow well fixed for life. My great-great-grandfather won the greatest and most hard-fought battle of his life in that hotel cottage parlor, and thus set in motion the chain of events that resulted in my writing this essay.

So, as you read about the many houses of America's presidents in this volume, try to imagine the houses that are not here as well. This will give you some sense of the richness of the history of the American home, and the irreplaceable value of the historic houses that do survive, offering us windows into our shared past.

Ulysses Grant Dietz,
Curator of Decorative Arts, and
Curator of The Ballantine House,
The Newark Museum, Newark, New Jersey

Homes of the Presidents of the United States

George Washington Birthplace National Monument
RR. 1, Box 717
Washington's Birthplace, Virginia 22443
(804) 224-1732

Features include the birthplace site, memorial house, Visitor Center, herb and flower gardens, living farm, walking trail, burial ground, and picnic area. Educational packets are available for use by teachers. Administered by the National Park Service.

The birthplace of the first president of the United States is a lovely setting overlooking Popes Creek, situated just south of the Potomac River. Nothing remains of the U-shaped house in which George Washington was born on February 22, 1732 – it was destroyed by fire on December 25, 1779. However, the pastoral setting where George Washington spent the first three and one-half years of his life remains intact. Looking out over the shimmering waters of Popes Creek (named for Nathaniel Pope, the President's great-great-grandfather), it is easy to see what drew George Washington's ancestors to this Tidewater region. Aside from its natural beauty, the region was also a fertile growing place for vegetables, corn, wheat, and perhaps most importantly, tobacco, which in 17th and 18th-century colonial America served as a substitute for currency. Here George Washington, who earned his reputation as a soldier and statesman, spent his early years learning the virtues and hardships of life on a farm. Throughout his life, his love of farming was never to diminish.

Later, the plantation was passed on to George Washington's nephew, William Augustine Washington. On Christmas Day, 1779, the house was lost to a fire and William Augustine moved away from the plantation. The house was never rebuilt.

Mount Vernon
Mount Vernon, Virginia 22121
(703) 780-2000

Features include the mansion, outbuildings, gardens, tomb of George and Martha Washington, slave burial ground, Mount Vernon Museum, snack bar, Mount Vernon Inn (restaurant), Museum Shop, Inn Gift Shop, post office, restrooms, greenhouse shop, information kiosk, first aid center, and historical trail to be used for hikes by scouting organizations. Administered by the Mount Vernon Ladies' Association.

Washington was to occupy many other dwellings as Commander-in-Chief of the Continental Army and as the first president of the United States, but throughout his long career, Mount Vernon was the only place George Washington truly regarded as home.

During his presidency, George Washington managed to visit Mount Vernon on 15 occasions, and yearned for the time when he could return to his beloved home and the tranquility of life as a private citizen. The time came for him in 1797, when after completing his second term as president, he was able to turn the office over to John Adams and return to life as a gentleman farmer. He spent the two and one-half years that remained to him at Mount Vernon, and died there, in his own bedroom, on December 14, 1799. Two and one-half years later, his wife Martha Washington also died and was entombed in the old family vault beside her husband. George Washington's will directed that a new brick tomb be built at a specific location at Mount Vernon to replace the old vault, which badly needed repairs. It was not until 1831 that it was completed and the bodies of George and Martha Washington were moved there, along with the remains of other family members. The tomb is surrounded by a brick wall and the bodies of George and Martha Washington are each encased in marble sarcophagi presented in 1837. The graves of other family members, as well as the Mount Vernon slave burial ground, are close by. The tomb, the restored vault, and the slave burial ground may be viewed by visitors to Mount Vernon today.

Deshler-Morris House
5442 Germantown Avenue
Philadelphia, Pennsylvania 19144
(215) 596-1748

This site features the house and gardens. Guided tour of site normally lasts about three-quarters of an hour. Administered by Deshler-Morris House Committee, in cooperation with the National Park Service.

In the summer of 1793, while Philadelphia was the capital of the United States, yellow fever struck the city. The pestilence was so virulent that most of the executive branch of the government, including President Washington himself, was forced to leave the city after having stayed in town only during the first days of September. President Washington spent most

MOUNT VERNON.

of the next two months of that year at Mount Vernon, and by late October, he made plans to return as close to the seat of government as he could manage. He rented the home of Colonel Isaac Franks, situated in Germantown, approximately seven miles north of Philadelphia. Arrangements to rent the house had been made by Attorney General Edmund Randolph, and of the three houses suggested by Randolph, President Washington chose Colonel Franks' house because it was "more commodious for myself and the entertainment of company."

Today, this house, named Deshler-Morris House in honor of its first and last private owners, stands as the earliest "White House" still in existence.

DESHLER-MORRIS HOUSE.

Adams National Historical Park
   John Adams & John Quincy Adams Birthplaces
   133-141 Franklin Street
   Quincy, Massachusetts 02169
   (617) 770-1175

The site features two houses, Visitor Center (in Quincy), and the United First Parish Church Center (where both presidents are buried). A bus provides transportation between sites. Administered by the National Park Service.

President John Adams was born on October 30, 1735, on a site that was originally part of a 140-acre plot. The house, which today has 133 Franklin Street as its address, was built c. 1681 and, like the adjacent birthplace of John Quincy Adams, is a saltbox structure with a central chimney. It is framed with huge beams, which are joined and secured by wood pegs, and has two-foot-wide planks in its floor and brick-filled walls. It originally had two lower and two upper rooms, but John Adams' father, Deacon John Adams, added a rear lean-to onto the house in 1744, expanding the space to include two more downstairs rooms and two small upstairs rooms, as well as a large attic. It was in this attic that the Deacon practiced his trade of cordwaining (shoemaking). During the day, while John's father tilled the fields, his mother, Susanna Boylston Adams, set about the dangerous business of preparing meals, utilizing the large fireplace which leads to the central chimney. In addition to its usefulness for hearth-cooking, the central chimney provided fireplaces that heated the other rooms in the house. This house was the home of President John Adams throughout his formative years, during his period of study at Harvard (he graduated in 1755), and during his early adult life while he taught school at Worcester, Massachusetts, and then studied law.

The adjacent house at 141 Franklin Street, where John Quincy Adams was born on July 11, 1767, was purchased by Deacon John Adams in 1744 and inherited by his son, John Adams, in 1761. Built in 1663, this saltbox structure was where Deacon Adams' son, John Adams, began married life with his wife, the former Abigail Smith. Like the birthplace of his father, John Quincy Adams' birthplace was originally a structure with a central chimney and two upper and two lower rooms, to which a lean-to was added for a new kitchen. John Adams came to use the original kitchen of this house as his law office. Abigail and John Adams lived in this house, which was their farm home, for interrupted periods between 1764, the year they married, and 1784, during which time they also resided in Boston, where John maintained a successful law practice. Their Boston homes included a rented house on Brattle Square, where they lived in 1768; a home on Cold Lane; and a house on Queen Street, which was theirs from 1772 to 1774.

In 1774, John Adams purchased his birthplace from his brother, who had acquired ownership, and sold both it and the birthplace of John Quincy Adams to his son in 1803. John Quincy Adams, his wife, Louisa Catherine Adams, and two of their children resided there until 1806. Both homes are now administered by the National Park Service, having been owned alternatively by the Adams family and the city of Quincy previously. Both houses were restored in 1982. They are the oldest presidential birthplaces, and the only birthplaces where two presidents were born 75 feet apart!

**Adams National Historic Site
  (The Old House)
  135 Adams Street
  Quincy, Massachusetts 02269
  (617) 770-1175**

Features include the home, library, garden, and carriage house. A Visitor Center (in Quincy Center) has a bookstore, exhibits, and restrooms. Administered by the National Park Service.

This gracious home, situated upon approximately forty acres of land at the time it was acquired by John and Abigail Adams in 1787 for 600 pounds, was the homestead of one of America's most prominent and influential families for four generations. Originally named "Peacefield" by John Adams, and later known as "The Old House," the structure was built by Major Leonard Vassall, a West Indian sugar planter. Originally, the house contained a paneled room, south entry, and dining room on the first floor, two bedrooms on the second floor, and three smaller rooms in the attic. The servants' quarters and kitchen were housed in separate buildings, as was typical in the New England of John and Abigail Adams.

THOMAS JEFFERSON

Tuckahoe Plantation
12601 River Road
Richmond, Virginia 23233
(804) 784-5736

Owned and operated by the Thompson Family, the site is open by appointment only. Features include the house, plantation, street and grounds. A one-room schoolhouse designed by Peter Jefferson, father of Thomas Jefferson, is on the site and is currently used as a gift shop.

Thomas Jefferson began his remarkable life on April 13, 1743, at Shadwell, located near Charlottesville, Virginia. He was the son of Peter Jefferson, a surveyor, and the former Jane Randolph, whose family was one of the most prominent families of colonial Virginia. Young Thomas Jefferson spent the first two years of his life at Shadwell, then word reached Peter Jefferson that William Randolph, first cousin of Jane Randolph Jefferson and master of the Tuckahoe Plantation, had met an untimely death at the age of thirty-two. As provided in a codicil to William Randolph's will, Peter Jefferson and his family, including two-year old Thomas, journeyed to Tuckahoe to care for William Randolph's two daughters and one son. Thus, Thomas Jefferson came to spend his formative years at Tuckahoe, living there with his family from 1745 to 1752.

Located seven miles west of Richmond, Virginia, Tuckahoe Plantation is the only surviving estate among the five established by the sons of William Randolph of Turkey Island, the first of the Randolphs to settle in colonial Virginia. Just when Tuckahoe was founded is subject to debate, with dates ranging from 1674 to 1730. However, there is no doubt that Tuckahoe is one of America's earliest architecturally significant frame houses, and incorporates some of the finest examples of early Georgian architecture. Such features include: a two room and central hall plan, so named because each floor of each wing of the house contains two large rooms separated by a stair hall. The "H" shape of the home, the product of adding wings to the original house, was popular in colonial Virginia, and similar in shape to the Capitol in Williamsburg and to Stratford Hall, the Lee family home in the Tidewater region. However, the fact that Tuckahoe is of frame construction, rather than brick or stone, makes it a truly unusual colonial-era home. The house also features four chimneys, each placed at the end of the large rooms, thus allowing for heat in the colder months, while parallel doors in the central hallway allow for cross-ventilation in the warmer months. It is said that Thomas Jefferson's interest in Palladian architecture, evidenced at his later homes in Monticello and Poplar Forest, was quite possibly sparked by his childhood admiration of the architectural features at Tuckahoe.

Monticello
P.O. Box 316
Charlottesville, Virginia 22902
(804) 984-9800

Monticello features the main house, a walking trail, flower and vegetable gardens, plant and museum shops, orchards, ruins of joinery, grave site, picnic area, rest rooms, and "Little Mountain Luncheonette." A nearby Visitors Center, located on State Route 20, includes an exhibition called "Thomas Jefferson at Monticello," which includes family memorabilia, architectural models and drawings and other items related to Thomas Jefferson's activities while at Monticello. Administered by the Thomas Jefferson Memorial Foundation, Inc.

A visit to Monticello is more than a discovery of the life and times of an important historical figure. It is a journey into the mind of one of the greatest thinkers of his time. Monticello is a testament to Thomas Jefferson's cleverness and diversity of interests. His talents and interests encompassed a range far beyond his gifts as a politician and statesman. At Monticello, whose name derives from an Italian word meaning "little mountain," we see the work of Thomas Jefferson the architect, the innovator, the aesthete and the farmer.

Thomas Jefferson chose this site himself. At an elevation of 867 feet, the view from Monticello encompasses Shadwell, the home where he was born on April 13, 1743. He chose the location as a lad, across the Rivanna River, because at the age of 14, he inherited approximately 3,000 acres from his father, Peter Jefferson, a farmer and surveyor. The elder Mr. Jefferson purchased the farm land in 1736, and one thousand acres of that land became Monticello.

Thomas Jefferson's Poplar Forest
Forest, Virginia 24551-0419
(804) 525-1806   www.poplarforest.org

Features here are the main house, original privies, museum shop and restrooms. There are archaeological excavation and restoration exhibits. Administered by The Corporation for Jefferson's Poplar Forest.

Poplar Forest, home of a well-known president, remains virtually unknown to the public. Thankfully, it escaped the threat of destruction through the foresight of private citizens who purchased the house and remaining acreage in 1984 as development encroached. Today, the exterior of the house has been restored to its original Jeffersonian design, an octagonal design hailed by many as one of Jefferson's finest.

The site of Poplar Forest, located southwest of Lynchburg, Virginia, was originally a 4,812-acre parcel that Jefferson and his wife Martha inherited when her father John Wayles died in 1773. Thomas Jefferson subsequently inherited the property when his wife died at the age of 33 years.

TUCKAHOE PLANTATION.

MONTICELLO.

POPLAR FOREST.

13

Montpelier
11407 Constitution Highway
Montpelier Station, Virginia 22957
(540) 672-2728   www.montpelier.org

Montpelier features the mansion, exhibits, an introductory video, and a landscaped walk. The walk has stops at the Madison family cemetery (final resting place of James and Dolley), Mount Pleasant site (original Madison family settlement at Montpelier, c. 1723) and other archaeological sites: a slave cemetery, ice temple, landscape arboretum, and restored gardens. An audio tour system is keyed to stops in the Mansion and on the walk. Self-guided trails can be found in the James Madison Landmark Forest (200-acre old growth forest, with trees up to 250 years old). Administered by the National Trust for Historic Preservation.

After many years of private ownership, the principal home of President James Madison is open to the public. The original estate was the result of a patent obtained by Thomas Chew and Ambrose Madison, James Madison's grandfather, for 4,675 acres of land in what is currently known as Orange County, Virginia. It was divided into equal shares for Mr. Madison and Mr. Chew.

The Montpelier Mansion, Georgian in design, was built by James Madison, Sr., the president's father, who served as justice of the peace and sheriff in Orange County in addition to being a successful planter, building contractor, and ironworks proprietor. The house was completed around 1760, but underwent significant renovations under Madison, Jr.'s watchful eye.

When James Madison, Sr. died in 1801, his son James inherited the Montpelier estate. The younger Madison's knowledge of architecture had already led him to add Tuscan columns and a portico to the house by 1800. The bases of the Tuscan columns originally began at the first floor level of the mansion, which is above ground level at the front of the mansion, where a stairway leads to the entrance. (A subsequent owner, Frank Carson, had the columns extended to the ground.) From 1809 to 1812, major additions were made to the house, including one-story wings with basement kitchens on either side of the house, as well as a Tuscan colonnade to the rear, extending outward from a porch which features three triple-hung windows. These windows reach to the floor and are designed to permit a person inside the mansion to raise the two lower sashes and step through the opening as though walking through a door. Other renovations also contributed to the mansion's transformation from its previous Georgian-style appearance into a Neoclassical style.

In 1983, the 2,700-acre estate was acquired by the National Trust for Historic Preservation. After a concerted effort to prepare the site for tours, Montpelier was opened to the public in 1987, allowing visitors to view the principal home of the author of the Bill of Rights.

MONTPELIER AS IT APPEARED PRIOR TO RESTORATION TO ITS APPEARANCE IN PRESIDENT MADISON'S TIME.

Ash Lawn-Highland
James Monroe Parkway
Charlottesville, Virginia 22902-8722

This site features the house, gardens, slave quarters, gift shop, restrooms, with bus and picnic facilities. Lund and Virginia wine tasting are both available by reservation. Administered by the College of William and Mary.

With the exception of the White House, Ash Lawn-Highland, known in James Monroe's day as Highland, is the only one of President Monroe's various residences which is both extant and open to the public daily. The house and grounds appear to maintain the simple charm that they must have had under Monroe's ownership. James Monroe, never a wealthy man, fought alongside George Washington in the Revolutionary War (the famous painting of the crossing of the Delaware includes a depiction of young Lieutenant James Monroe holding the American flag). He had held numerous public offices (more than any other president before or since) when he purchased the 1,000-acre farm and estate in 1793 for a cost of $1.00 per acre. Monroe had two significant reasons for purchasing the farm: his aspiration to purchase an income-generating property he believed could produce 20,000 pounds of tobacco a year, and the mutual desire of James Monroe and his friend Thomas Jefferson to become neighbors in Albemarle County. Monroe met Jefferson while the latter was Governor of Virginia, and the two men quickly became friends. Monroe then began to study law under Jefferson.

Thomas Jefferson assisted his friend by selecting the site for the house and loaning his gardener to plant the orchard. Jefferson also helped to plan the house, which is an example of vernacular architecture, as befitted the limited funds available at the time. Remodeled and enlarged over the years, the frame house includes a two-story frame structure built in 1882 by the Massey family over Monroe foundations, with the original Monroe one-story wing extending to the west. Beneath the wing are a kitchen and, on the south, a gallaried porch. Even as remodeled, the house maintains a character that stands in stark contrast to the Palladian classicism of Monticello or the Georgian splendor of Mount Vernon. It retains the rectitude of its original owner, who wanted a "cabin-castle" befitting the life of a farmer.

Oak Hill Farm
Aldie, Virginia
(703) 777-1246

Owned by Mr. and Mrs. Thomas H. De Lashmutt. Open for special events only. Please call for further information. Features found here are the house and grounds.

During his second term as president, James Monroe decided to make Loudoun County, Virginia, where he and his uncle, Judge Joseph Jones of Fredericksburg, had purchased property in 1794, the site of his permanent seat. A man of modest origins who believed firmly that one's home should reflect one's station in life, President Monroe determined to build a home for his family that would reflect his well-earned stature in society. Construction of that home, a stately brick structure that came to be known as Oak Hill, began in 1822 and was completed in 1823. It is said that the name was derived from thirteen trees, a gift from Congress representing the thirteen states, which Monroe planted on the property. At first, it served as a convenient summer home for President Monroe and his family because of its proximity to Washington, but after President Monroe left office it became his retirement home.

ASH LAWN-HIGHLAND.

OAK HILL FARM.

Museum of the Waxhaws & Andrew Jackson Memorial
   Highway 75 East
   Waxhaw, North Carolina 28173
   (704) 843-1832

Site in North Carolina features a historic marker, and a museum containing military and Jackson related artifacts. Andrew Jackson State Park, in South Carolina, features trails, camp sites, and boat rentals available for fishing. Administered by the Division of Archives and History, Department of Cultural Resources, State of North Carolina.

ANDREW JACKSON STATE PARK IN SOUTH CAROLINA.

North Carolina and South Carolina each claim to contain the birthplace site of the hero of the Battle of New Orleans, and America's seventh chief executive, within its borders. Both states also have stone markers commemorating President Jackson's birth. The South Carolina marker cites a letter, written by Andrew Jackson himself, stating that he was born on "James Crawford's plantation," historically shown as having been located in Lancaster County, South Carolina. The North Carolina marker, the older of the two stone markers, includes a carved depiction of a log cabin and a declaration that it marks the actual site of Andrew Jackson's birth. South Carolina's marker makes no such claim, but in apparent contradiction to the North Carolina marker, stresses that Andrew Jackson "himself" was told that he was born "on South Carolina soil."

The controversy over the place of Andrew Jackson's birth stems from confusion over what the colonial boundaries were in 1767, and disagreement concerning where Jackson's mother was staying at the time of his birth. She appears to have worked at James Crawford's plantation about the time Andrew Jackson was born but others believe that Andrew's mother was visiting a sister's home in North Carolina when the future president was born. Either way, Andrew Jackson spent his early life, between 1767 and 1781, almost exclusively in the Waxhaw area.

The Hermitage
   4580 Rachel's Lane
   Hermitage, Tennessee 37076
   (615) 889-2941   www.thehermitage.com

This site features an audio tour of mansion and grounds. The Visitor Center has a museum, store, restaurant, and a theater which shows a film presentation about the Jacksons and The Hermitage. The grounds also include a smokehouse, garden, cemetery, the "Original Hermitage," Tulip Grove Mansion, church, and a Confederate cemetery. Owned and administered by the Ladies Hermitage Association.

After living at two other Tennessee plantations (Poplar Grove and Hunter's Hill), Andrew Jackson purchased the land that would become The Hermitage in 1804. It was a 425-acre tract within two miles of Andrew and Rachel Jackson's previous plantation at Hunter's Hill. By February of 1805, the Jacksons were occupying their home on this tract. It was a square log home with four rooms, a large room downstairs and three bedrooms upstairs. The downstairs room was used as a parlor and sitting room. Nearby were three smaller log homes, each one story in height, which may have been used to accommodate guests; at least one was housing for slaves. The log home was the home of Andrew and Rachel Jackson for 17 years.

It appears to have been a happy home, where the couple lived together with Rachel Jackson's nephew (whom the Jacksons adopted and renamed Andrew Jackson, Jr.) and from 1817 onward, their ward, A. J. Hutchings. The senior Andrew Jackson's duties as general of the U.S. Army during the War of 1812 and later, his presidency, meant prolonged absences from his home. During these absences, the farm was operated by one or more of Rachel Jackson's brothers with the aid of overseers.

THE HERMITAGE.

MARTIN VAN BUREN

Martin Van Buren National Historic Site (Lindenwald)
1013 Old Post Road
Kinderhook, New York 12106
(518) 758-9689   www.ups.gov\mava

Lindenwald features the restored mansion and farm, ex-hibits, a gift concession, and a 10-minute video presenta-tion on Van Buren. Tours are offered throughout the day. Please begin your visit at the Visitor Center located across Old Post Road from the visitor parking lot. Administered by the National Park Service.

The man who came to be known as the "Red Fox of Kinderhook," was born in a tavern on December 5, 1782. The tavern, which was demolished in the late 1800s, was a clap-board building with a small kitchen annex. It was owned by Martin Van Buren's father, Abraham, a respected landowner and farmer in the small town of Kinderhook, located about 25 miles south of Albany on the east side of the Hudson River.

While secretary of state from 1829 to 1831, Van Buren was a tenant in the Stephen Decatur House, a red brick Federal-style home designed by Benjamin Henry Latrobe and built in 1819 for Commodore Stephen Decatur, renowned for his victories in the War of 1812 and in the Barbary Wars. After Commodore Decatur was killed in a duel in 1820, Mrs. Susan Decatur rented the elegant town house to Van Buren and a host of other distin-guished men, including Secretaries of State Henry Clay and Edward Livingston. It is said that during Mr. Van Buren's resi-dence there, he cut a window in the wall on the garden side of the house in order to relay signals to President Jackson at the nearby White House. Today, Decatur House, located at 748 Jack-son Place, N.W., Washington, D.C., is a property of the National Trust for Historic Preservation and is open to the public.

In 1837, Martin Van Buren succeeded Andrew Jackson to the presidency. After two years in the White House, President Van Buren, looking ahead to his retirement, purchased the 130-acre Lindenwald estate for $14,000. However, his retirement was to come sooner than he expected, for he was defeated in his re-election bid by his Whig opponent, William Henry Harrison.

The Lindenwald mansion had already undergone extensive changes since the time of its original construction in 1797 as a simple, rectangular Georgian style home for Judge Peter Van Ness. By the time President Van Buren purchased the property, a classical ballroom had been added. Van Buren, however, wanted to convert his estate to a working farm. By 1845, it was complete, with flower gardens, ornamental fishponds, wooden fences and outbuildings. Van Buren also had indoor plumbing installed in the house, including a flush toilet and bathtub in which he bathed every day. The kitchen wing also included pumps and plumbing, a coal range and a brick oven.

Martin Van Buren's changes to the mansion itself were even more dramatic. He removed its central stairway and expanded the rooms on both floors of the house. He added 51 French wallpaper panels, depicting a hunting scene, to the expanded downstairs hall. These panels were removed in 1977 and rehung in 1987. Sixty percent of the furnishings on display in the mansion today belonged to Mr. Van Buren and/or his family.

Van Buren's son, Smith Thompson Van Buren, agreed to move into Lindenwald in 1849 to help manage the estate, and was given license to redesign the house as he saw fit, for him-self and his family. Consequently, Smith Thompson Van Buren sought out architect Richard Upjohn, who designed Trinity Church in lower Manhattan. Mr. Upjohn's architectural changes were profound: he added 18 rooms to the house, a front porch and other exterior features reflecting the Gothic and Ro-manesque styles and a four-story Italianate tower at the rear of the house. Smith Thompson Van Buren added the crowning touch by having the house painted yellow, resulting in a eclec-tic-looking structure with three stories and 36 rooms.

Martin Van Buren had bedrooms on the second floor for himself and his children, including: Abraham, whose wife, An-gelica, acted as hostess in the Van Buren White House and was a cousin of Dolly Madison; Martin, Jr.; John; and Smith Th-ompson. These rooms have low ceilings and feature sleigh beds of Empire or Classical design. His room contains the bed in which he died of bronchial asthma in 1862.

After the president's death, the house went through a vari-ety of uses, including: a tea house, a nursing home, an antique shop, and theatrical quarters, before the purchase of the man-sion and 22 of the surrounding acres by the United States gov-ernment in 1976.

Berkeley Plantation
   Charles City, Virginia 23030
   (804) 829-6018

Berkeley features costumed guides conducting house tours, magnificent gardens overlooking the James River, the highly acclaimed Coach House Tavern, and a gift shop. Privately owned by Malcolm E. Jamieson.

This historic plantation was the scene of many "firsts," including Virginia's celebration of the first official Thanksgiving in 1619 and the composition of *Taps* by General Daniel Butterfield of the Army of the Potomac in 1862. The ninth president of the United States, William Henry Harrison was born here on February 9, 1773. His grandfather, Benjamin Harrison, had constructed the early Georgian mansion in 1726. His father, Benjamin Harrison V, a signer of the Declaration of Independence, was also born at Berkeley.

The plantation house is a three-story Georgian brick structure, with a great hall surrounded by two rooms on each side on the first floor, and a full basement where a film presentation on the history of Berkeley is shown.

In 1907, John Jamieson of Scotland, a former drummer boy in General McClellan's army during the occupation of Berkeley, discovered that the plantation was for sale. Needing a valuable source of timber to be used in constructing New York Harbor, he purchased the 1,400-acre plantation for $28,000. The plantation house, thought valueless, was included as part of the sale at no additional cost. Mr. Jamieson's son, Malcolm Jamieson, endeavored successfully to restore the plantation home and grounds to the glory of its days as the Harrison family seat

William Henry Harrison, the first president to campaign actively for his high office, returned to Berkeley in 1841 to write his lengthy inaugural address. He delivered the speech outdoors in a freezing rain on March 4, 1841, and within one month he was dead. (At 69, he was our second oldest president). Forty-seven years later, his grandson, Benjamin Harrison, was elected as the 23rd president of the United States, making Berkeley Plantation the ancestral home of two American presidents. It is fortunate that Berkeley remains preserved and flourishes, thanks to the efforts of the Jamieson family.

Grouseland
   3 West Scott Street
   Vincennes, Indiana 47591
   (812) 882-2096

Features of this site are the mansion, Visitor Center, gift and book shops. Administered by the Francis Vigo Chapter of the National Society of the Daughters of the American Revolution.

In 1801, William Henry Harrison, while governor of the Indiana Territory, wanted to build a home reminiscent of his birthplace at Berkeley Plantation. He purchased 300 acres of cleared land on the banks of the Wabash River. During 1803 and 1804, Governor Harrison built a hand-made brick home in the modified Federal style. His love of hunting grouse inspired the name of his new home – Grouseland.

Grouseland mansion was the Harrison abode from 1804 to 1812. William Henry Harrison left Grouseland in 1812 to become Commander-in-Chief of the Northwest Territory, during which time he fought in Canada in the Battle of the Thames. His military successes during this time, as well as his career in Indiana when he led the territorial forces in the famous Battle of Tippecanoe, made him a military hero throughout the United States and provided impetus for his subsequent career in politics.

JOHN TYLER

Sherwood Forest Plantation
14501 John Tyler Memorial Parkway
Charles City, Virginia 23030
(804) 829-5377

Sherwood Forest features guided tours of main rooms in the Big House, and a self-guided tour of plantation grounds with marked points of interest. Privately owned by President Tyler's grandson and his family.

This beautiful mansion and grounds are unique because they are still owned and managed by descendants of a former United States president. Sherwood Forest was so named by President John Tyler because of his treatment as an "outlaw" by the Whig Party. The mansion, built c. 1730 on a 1,200-acre estate, had fallen into disrepair when Tyler purchased it in 1842 for $10,000. By 1844, Tyler had the Georgian clapboard structure renovated by connecting the central structure to two smaller buildings on either side. Some 301 feet long, it is the longest frame house in America.

Before purchasing Sherwood Forest, Tyler attended the College of William and Mary, boarding with his brother-in-law, Judge James Semple. While his father was governor of Virginia, John Tyler apprenticed at the law office of Edmund Randolph. In 1809, he began practicing law in Charles City County. He married Letitia Christian in 1813, and honeymooned at the Greenbriar Cottage in White Sulphur Springs (now in West Virginia). The couple settled at Mons-Sacer, a 500-acre section of the Greenway, the estate on which President Tyler was born on March 29, 1790. The home on this 1,200-acre estate, which President Tyler later inherited, is a story and a half frame house, which has a brick basement, dormers and outside chimneys. Today, the house is privately owned.

Between 1811 and 1834, John Tyler served intermittent terms in the Virginia House of Delegates. He also served in the United States House of Representatives beginning at age 26, and lived in a boarding house while in government service. In 1821, he lived either at Woodburn, which he built in 1811, or at Greenway in Charles City. He was governor of Virginia from 1825 to 1827, residing in the executive mansion. He became a United States senator in 1828, serving in that capacity until 1836. During this period, he lived on a 600-acre farm on the York River in Gloucester County, Virginia. In 1837, he moved to a home on Francis Street in Williamsburg, Virginia. This home, which was his until 1841, was later demolished.

In 1841, John Tyler became president after the unexpected death of the ninth president, William Henry Harrison. While in office, he used "Woodley" at 3000 Cathedral Avenue in Washington as a summer home (as had his predecessor Martin Van Buren) and also summered at the Greenbriar Cottage in White Sulphur Springs, Virginia (now West Virginia). From 1853 to 1858, years after he left office, he summered at

"Villa Margaret," at the beach at Old Point Comfort, Hampton, Virginia. He first rented, and then bought, this beach home.

Tragically, President Tyler's wife of 29 years, Letitia Christian Tyler, died in 1842, the year he purchased Sherwood Forest. President Tyler made Sherwood Forest home for himself and his new bride, Julia Gardiner of Gardiner's Island, New York, whom he married while in office, the first president to do so. In purchasing the Charles City plantation, Tyler selected a location near his birthplace at Greenway. His enjoyment of the plantation began in earnest in 1845 at the end of his term of office. He became active in the secessionist movement, served in the ill-fated Peace Convention of 1861, and at the time of his death on January 18, 1862, was a member of the Confederate Congress. The Confederate Congress met in Richmond, and while serving there, the former president stayed at the Ballard House and later at the Exchange Hotel.

President Tyler's quieter years at Sherwood Forest were earned by a turbulent term in office. He became the first vice president to clearly establish the precedent of presidential succession upon the death of President William Henry Harrison in 1841. Because the Constitution makes reference to the authority of a vice president to act as the president should the president be unable to perform his duties, it was, at the time, arguable whether the vice president had clear Constitutional authority to succeed a deceased president. President Tyler, however, did take the oath of office and succeed Harrison, a source of outrage to Senator Henry Clay, whose presidential ambitions were undisguised, and other Whig Party leaders. The dispute created a rift between Tyler and the Whig Party that never healed, and led to the resignation of Tyler's entire "inherited" cabinet, except Daniel Webster. President Tyler filled the vacuum of this mass resignation by appointing John C. Calhoun and other talented statesmen. Despite such political strife, Tyler achieved the annexation of Texas by the end of his administration.

Today, Sherwood Forest is owned by the family of Harrison Tyler, the president's grandson, and remains in appearance much as it did during the days of President Tyler.

James K. Polk Memorial State Historic Site (Birthplace)
  Box 475
  Pineville, North Carolina 28134
  (704) 889-7145

Features include a marker commemorating the birthplace of James K. Polk, replicas of President Polk's birthplace and a kitchen house, a Visitor Center, museum, gift shop, and rest rooms. Guided tours and a movie are included. Administered by the Division of Archives and History, Department of Cultural Resources, State of North Carolina.

The eleventh president of the United States, James Knox Polk was born of Scottish Presbyterian stock in what is now Pineville in Mecklenburg County, North Carolina. Great-uncle Thomas Polk, first of the Polk family to come to the area from Pennsylvania, was a founder of Mecklenburg. Thomas's father, William Polk, followed his son to North Carolina from Pennsylvania with the rest of the Polk family. William's other son, Ezekiel Polk, was the father of Samuel Polk, who married Jane Knox. On November 2, 1795, Jane Knox Polk gave birth to a son, James Knox Polk.

Young James Polk lived at the Polk plantation with his three siblings until the age of eleven. During that time, Samuel Polk prospered as a land surveyor, and ran a successful cotton and corn plantation on 250 acres of land, where young James learned much about farm life. Although the Polks lived in a log home, it was a spacious, two-story structure with a separate kitchen house. Fenced enclosures for livestock were situated nearby, and Sugar Creek was a ready source of water. About five slaves lived on the plantation, carrying on the day-to-day work. Living under these conditions, the Polks were considered a prosperous family in their community.

Twenty-one acres of the Polk birthplace have been acquired by the state of North Carolina. A marker in the shape of a pyramid, erected in 1904, commemorates the birthplace. Replicas of the Polk birthplace and kitchen house, both filled with furnishings of the early 1800s, stand on the site, which includes a Visitors Center, and a museum where a 25-minute film on Polk's life is shown. The site is also ideal for picnics and nature hikes.

James K. Polk Ancestral Home
  301 West 7th Street
  Columbia, Tennessee 38401
  (931) 388-4164

Features: Main house, kitchen house, gardens, and adjacent sisters' house (which includes museum, video presentation, gift shop, and rest rooms). Administered by the James K. Polk Memorial Association.

The James K. Polk Ancestral Home is the only home President Polk ever lived in, besides the White House, which remains extant. It was built in 1816, while James Polk was attending the University of North Carolina at Chapel Hill, by James Polk's father, Samuel Polk, whose entrepreneurial and surveying activities drew him to move into Columbia and away from the farm that had been his home for the previous ten years. The James K. Polk Ancestral Home is a two-story brick structure of the Federal style popular in Tennessee in 1816.

POLK'S BIRTHPLACE.

Springfield
   5608 Apache Road
   Louisville, Kentucky 40207
   (502) 897-9990

Privately owned by Dr. William C. Gist. If contacted in advance, Dr. Gist will arrange tours of his house. This section is dedicated to the memory of Betty Gist, whose devotion to American history will not be forgotten.

In the spring of 1785, infant Zachary Taylor came with his family to "Springfield," the 400-acre Taylor family farm in the Beargrass Creek region near Louisville, Kentucky. The property, located in Jefferson County, Kentucky, was east of the Louisville city limits. A prominent and well-to-do family, the Taylors had lived at Hare Forest, a plantation near Culpeper, Orange County, Virginia. Colonel Taylor, Zachary Taylor's father, sold Hare Forest in 1784 and set forth with his family and slaves to find a new home. On the journey, measles broke out and the Taylor party had to be quarantined immediately. The Taylors secured temporary lodgings on a plantation called Montebello, near Barbourville, in Orange County, Virginia. It was at Montebello that Zachary Taylor, third son and third child of Colonel Taylor and Sarah Dabney Strother Taylor (who had nine children in all; the first six were sons — then three daughters) was born on November 24, 1784. It is thought that the Taylors lived in log outbuildings while at Montebello, but the original buildings no longer exist. Leaving his wife and three young sons at Montebello, Colonel Taylor journeyed on to Kentucky with his slaves to establish the new Taylor home at Springfield. In 1785, he brought his family to their new home, where they continued to be well-regarded and successful. The Springfield property later expanded to 700 acres, and, according to early 19th century tax records, Colonel Taylor came to own about 10,000 acres of property in seven Kentucky counties. Of their nine children, eight survived into adulthood.

Zachary Taylor spent most of the first 23 years of his life at Springfield. The original home, built by the Colonel and his slaves, was a log cabin which was later moved to the back of the property for slave quarters. It was replaced by the current structure, a large two and a half story Georgian Colonial red brick, Flemish bond house, constructed in a style similar to a Virginia plantation home between 1785 and 1790. The bricks used to build it were fired on the Springfield property. It was a comfortable manor home for the Taylor family, with two rooms on each floor and featuring walnut wood and ash flooring. Between 1810 and 1820, a second side of the house was built. It also had two rooms on each floor and ash flooring, but had wider mantels and larger fireplaces. The wood on the newer side of the house was painted, rather than walnut stained like the older side of the house.

In 1981 the house was purchased as a private residence by Dr. William Gist, former president general of the National Society of the Sons of the American Revolution, active in historical and genealogical organizations, and noted researcher on the history of the house and the life of Zachary Taylor. He has acquired furnishings and articles dating to the period when the Taylors lived there, and occasionally discovers artifacts on the property that may have been used by the Taylors, including a spoon that seems to be made of nickel alloy or coin silver made c. 1800-1810. Other artifacts include 19th century coins and animal teeth. Dr. Gist is particularly proud of a c. 1810 white upholstered Sheraton sofa. He also owns an early, American secretary from roughly the same time period. A 1793 Pennsylvania tall case clock stands in the hall. In the dining room are an 1807 cherry sideboard and dining table, once owned by friends of the Taylors, so it is likely that Zachary Taylor himself sat at this table. Dr. Gist also owns a square grand piano made in Louisville in 1848; the piano is still in playable condition. Upstairs are seven rope beds made of either cherry or walnut with overshot coverlets in navy and white or red and white. These beds, which lend an informal look to the upstairs rooms, are similar to the beds the Taylors owned in the early 19th century. One piece of furniture is original — a simple rocking chair made of poplar, a yellowish wood. The chair, which documents establish was owned and used by the Taylors at Springfield, was donated to the house and will remain there. In November 1984, the Gists promoted the bicentennial of President Taylor's birth, and hosted a birthday party at Springfield in his honor, complete with cake and spice. Their efforts in promoting Zachary Taylor's 200th birthday earned them a letter of commendation from President Reagan in July 1985.

President Taylor, buried a short distance from Springfield at Zachary Taylor National Cemetery, would be pleased to see how well this home has been maintained. Although no longer the scene of a 700-acre plantation requiring the services of 52 slaves, the house is still a fine example of early American plantation architecture. The only extant building in which Zachary Taylor once lived has survived in excellent condition, and his boyhood home was the first building in Louisville and Jefferson County to be designated a historic landmark. His dying words, "I have endeavored to do my duty; my only regret is the friends I leave behind," sums up his life well, for his sense of duty and moral obligation, to his family, to his troops, and to his country, was the significant trait that made this otherwise modest man a great leader.

MILLARD FILLMORE

Millard Fillmore Birthplace (replica)
Glen State Park
16 86 Street Route 38
Moravia, New York 13118
(315) 497-0130

Glen State Park is 938 acres and features a replica of Fillmore's log cabin, 60 campsites and 3 cabins, swimming, hiking trails, playground, playing fields, picnic areas, showers, comfort stations and fishing. Administered by the State of New York Office of Parks, Recreation and Historic Preservation.

Millard Fillmore was a man of humble beginnings whose father had come from Vermont to settle in Locke Township, Cayuga County, New York. President Fillmore was born on January 7, 1800, in a modest log cabin built c. 1795. After a brief stay in this cabin, the Fillmores moved to a 100-acre leased farm in Sempronios, New York. Young Millard Fillmore grew up in relative isolation on that farm, with no neighbors closer than four miles away. The small farm cabin housed not only his immediate family, but also his aunt and uncle.

The original cabin, whose location is marked on Skinner Hill Road in present-day Summerhill, was destroyed in the 1840s. Just 5.7 miles west of that site, in Glen State Park, stands a replica of the birthplace cabin based on descriptions of the original. A "Swedish-style" 21 by 16-foot cabin chinked with mortar mixed with animal and human hair, it formerly stood on the John H. Rouse farm. In 1963, the Rouses donated it to the Millard Fillmore Memorial Association, which restored the cabin, largely through volunteer efforts. Its logs, which are ash, birch, elm and white pine, are the original cabin logs. The log rafters are held together with wooden pegs. The iron cut nails, hinges, door latch and fireplace crane were hand forged. Its chimney is fieldstone, taken from the Fillmore birthplace site. Its roof is hand-split red cedar from British Columbia.

The completed cabin, dedicated on May 23, 1965, is a two-room structure. Visitors enter and view the rooms through large glass windows, and can see items used by people of Millard Fillmore's time and circumstances, such as 19th-century farm machinery, a delft blue dining set, a high box bed, a small cradle, and a mirror to reflect light. A stone chimney and hearth, used for cooking and heating, and a bellows and candle molds are also found here. This cabin, and its simple furnishings, suggest the modest origins of the man who became the thirteenth president of the United States.

The Millard Fillmore House Museum
24 Shearer Avenue
East Aurora, New York 14052
(716) 652-4228

This site features a guided tour of the house by docents in period costumes. Administered by the Aurora Historical Society, Inc.

In 1826, Millard Fillmore, who had moved to Aurora (now East Aurora), New York and set up a law practice, married the former Abigail Powers. The Fillmores moved to a new home, built in part by Mr. Fillmore's own hands, across from his law office on Main Street. It was moved to the back of its lot on Main Street to make way for a theater. After years in disrepair, it caught the eye of Margaret Price, an artist and wife of Irving Price of Fisher-Price Toys. Fascinated with the house and its history, she purchased it in 1930, moved it to its present location on Shearer Avenue, and remodeled it to use as an art studio. In 1975, the house came to the attention of the Aurora Historical Society, which organized a fund-raising campaign and bought the house. The Society restored the house to its 1826-30 appearance, drawing upon recollections of older persons who remembered the interior of the house from childhood. A 1910 newspaper photo story was also a valuable source of information.

Franklin Pierce Homestead
Hillsboro, New Hampshire 03244
(603) 478-3165

The homestead features a 45-minute guided tour of the house. Administered by the Hillsboro Historical Society.

Franklin Pierce was born on November 23, 1804, in the vicinity of Hillsboro, New Hampshire. His father, Benjamin Pierce, had bought a log cabin and approximately 50 acres of land about one-half mile outside of Lower Village, and later constructed a small wood frame house on that site. It is unclear where Franklin Pierce was born; however, sometime shortly afterward, the family moved to the new home. It was a 10-room structure, painted on three sides only, to save money. After 20 or more years went by, it was painted red in back. Within another 20 years, a pre-existing two-story ell was rolled into place and added onto the rear of the house, perhaps replacing a temporary shed. For the first few years, Benjamin Pierce, who had a liquor license, operated the home as a tavern until his 200-acre site could be cleared for farming.

After studying at schools in Hancock and Francestown, Franklin Pierce went on to higher education at Bowdoin College in Brunswick, Maine, where he met Jane Means Appleton. Jane, who married Franklin Pierce, had family ties to Boston aristocracy, thereby assuring Mr. Pierce of his own place in society. In 1825, Mr. Pierce came to Portsmouth, New Hampshire, where he studied law.

At age 29 Franklin Pierce was elected to the New Hampshire state legislature. After two terms he was elected to the United States House of Representatives in 1833. While in Washington he boarded at a four-story brick house on Pennsylvania Avenue near Third. Franklin Pierce bought another house in Hillsboro a short distance from the mansion, but he spent little time at his new house, favoring the older mansion. Mrs. Pierce did not care much for Hillsboro, so after the death of their first son, the Pierces sold their house and moved to Concord. Franklin Pierce never lived in Hillsboro after that time but always thought of his place of birth as his one true home. The mansion was inherited by Pierce's oldest sister, and Mr. Pierce continued to visit her there, as well as call upon his brother and other friends and relatives in the Hillsboro area.

The Franklin Pierce Homestead was purchased by the state of New Hampshire in 1925. The state leases the site to the Hillsboro Historical Society, which makes the site available to visitors. Modern visitors realize that the Franklin Pierce Homestead is a mansion fit for a sizeable family. It is now yellow on three sides with green blinds; its back wall and barn are red, and it has two large fireplace chimneys and a two-story ell.

Pierce Manse
  14 Penacook Street
  Concord, New Hampshire 00301
  (603) 224-9620 / 7668

Features: Home and gift shop. Lecture and meeting room in basement, available for rent. Administered by the Pierce Brigade.

Resigning from the United States Senate to resume his law practice in Concord, New Hampshire, Franklin Pierce purchased a modest, two-story, Federal-style house in 1842. He moved in with his wife, Jane Means Appleton Pierce, and their two small sons, Franky and Benny. Their sojourn at this home was a mixture of success and tragedy. Before moving in, the Pierces had lost their first son, Franklin Pierce, Jr., a three-day old infant. In 1843, their second son, Franky, was born, but he died of typhus at the age of four in the Pierce home. Two months before his inauguration as president in 1853, Pierce's third son, Benny, was killed in a railroad accident. When President Pierce died in 1869, he left no heirs and no direct descendants.

While living here in Concord, Franklin Pierce's legal and political careers flourished. As a strong proponent of the Jacksonian Democrats, Mr. Pierce became widely respected in his party, largely because of his oratorical skills. Franklin Pierce was also a supporter of the territorial expansion of the United States, so when war with Mexico broke out in 1848 he quickly enlisted. He received a commission as brigadier general and acquired the reputation of a military hero as a result of his role in the war. By the time Franklin Pierce returned from his service in the Mexican War, he had determined to sell the Pierce Manse, probably because of the grief he and his wife shared over the loss of their son, Franky Pierce. For the next four years, the Pierces boarded at the home of a friend until Franklin received the presidential nomination.

The combination of his legal, political, and military experiences made him an attractive potential candidate for the presidency, and he received the nomination of the Democratic party for president in 1852. Winning the election, Franklin Pierce was soon plagued by accusations of being pro-slavery. In spite of this hinderance, he acquired 29,500 acres from Mexico (the Gadsden Purchase) to settle the desputed southern boundary of the United States.

The Pierce Manse remained privately owned long after Pierce's death, and was slated for demolition as part of an urban renewal project in 1966. In response to the threat, a group of citizens known as the Pierce Brigade was formed to preserve the building. The Brigade acquired the building itself, but was required to move the house from its original location at 18 Montgomery Street, in Concord's Historic District.

The Pierce Manse is currently administered by the Pierce Brigade, which has filled the home with furnishings and decor typical of Franklin Pierce's time. Stylistically, this large, white frame house is a blend of Federal-style features and aspects of the early Victorian era.

Buchanan's Log Cabin Birthplace
  Mercersburg Academy
  Mercersburg, PA 17236
  (717) 328-2151

Buchanan's Birthplace State Historical Park
  U.S. 16
  Mercersburg, PA 17236

These sites feature Buchanan's log cabin, a stone pyramid marking the birthplace, picnicking, and restrooms. Administered by the Commonwealth of Pennsylvania.

James Buchanan, the fifteenth president of the United States, was born at Stony Batter, near Mercersburg, Pennsylvania, on a site marked by a stone pyramid. The pyramid was conceived by Harriet Lane, the president's niece, who served as White House hostess for the bachelor president. Today the site upon which the Buchanan log cabin was originally located is an 18-acre state park. The cabin itself was moved to Fayette Street, Mercersburg, in 1850 and was used as a weaver shop. In 1925, the cabin was moved again to nearby Chambersburg and served as a gift shop and later as a Democratic headquarters. The cabin was purchased by the headmaster of the Mercersburg Academy in 1953 and brought to its campus. Its early American furnishings, while not original, suggest President Buchanan's humble origins in a one-room home.

Wheatland
  1120 Marietta Avenue
  Lancaster, Pennsylvania 17603
  (717) 392-8721   www.wheatland.org

This site features the mansion, 8-minute audio/visual presentation, museum exhibition, gift shops, refreshments, rest rooms, and picnic tables. Allow one hour for presentation and tour. Administered by the James Buchanan Foundation for the Preservation of Wheatland.

This lovely brick, Federal-style home is situated on four acres of land dominated by large, old trees and graced by a spacious lawn. When James Buchanan purchased the property in 1848, it contained 22 acres and a house built in 1828, for William Jenkins, a lawyer and banker. Wheatland is considered a fine example of Federal architecture.

James Buchanan, who lived at Wheatland while secretary of state, was a lifelong bachelor. He shared his residence with his nephew, James Buchanan Henry, who served as his personal secretary during the first two years of his administration, and his niece, Harriet Lane, who acted as mistress of Wheatland and as First Lady during her bachelor uncle's administration. Harriet Lane resided at Wheatland from the time her uncle left office in 1861 until 1866, when she married Harry Elliott Johnston and moved to Baltimore. When President Buchanan died in 1868, Harriet Lane Johnson inherited Wheatland and spent summers there until she sold the property in 1884. The house and estate remained in private hands until 1935, when it was sold to the James Buchanan Foundation for the Preservation of Wheatland. Wheatland was designated a National Historic Landmark in 1961.

Abraham Lincoln Birthplace
National Historic Site
2995 Lincoln Farm Road
Hodgenville, Kentucky 42748
(270) 358-3137
    Administered by the National Park Service.

Lincoln's Boyhood Home
U.S. 31E
Hodgenville, Kentucky 42748
(502) 549-3741
    Administered by Lincoln's Boyhood Home, Inc.

The Birthplace features a Visitor Center with exhibits, a film Lincoln: The Kentucky Years, *a memorial building containing a reconstructed "birth-place" cabin, Sinking Spring, hiking trails, picnic area, and rest rooms. The Boyhood Home has a reconstructed log cabin, gift shop/ museum, picnic grounds, log pavilion, and rest rooms.*

On December 12, 1808, Thomas Lincoln, former militiaman, carpenter, and general laborer, bought a 300-acre farm on the south fork of the Nolin River for $200 cash. At the time, Thomas Lincoln and his young wife, Nancy Hanks Lincoln, had

been married over two years and had a one-year old daughter, Sarah. Thomas Lincoln's ancestors had come from England by way of Virginia. His father, Abraham Lincoln, first made the journey to the Kentucky wilderness, but was killed by a Native American during a raid in May 1786. This left ten-year old Thomas to fend for himself and his family, and he learned self-reliance in the rugged Kentucky frontier. His reckless nature led him throughout Kentucky, until he finally settled at what later became known as Sinking Spring Farm. The limestone springs, from which the farm took its name, lie within a crevice in the earth and can still be seen. It was at Sinking Spring Farm on February 12, 1809, that Nancy Hanks Lincoln gave birth to a son, Abraham Lincoln.

In 1811, the Lincolns decided to leave Sinking Spring Farm to live at Knob Creek Farm, only a few miles away. They hoped to have better luck farming the land of Knob Creek, which they believed was better for raising crops. It was here that Abraham Lincoln spent five formative childhood years, and in manhood, he claimed that his earliest childhood memories were of Knob Creek Farm.

Lincoln Boyhood National Memorial
Box 1816
Lincoln City, Indiana 47552
(812) 937-4541
    Administered by the National Park Service.

Lincoln State Park
Box 216
Lincoln City, Indiana 47552
(812) 937-4710
    Administered by Indiana Dept. of Natural Resources.

Features: The Lincoln Boyhood National Memorial - Visitor Center with two memorial halls, exhibits, museum; the grave site of Nancy Hanks Lincoln (Abraham Lincoln's mother) and the Lincoln Living Historical Farm. The farm features the log buildings, animals and crops of a pioneer farm. Costumed "pioneers" carry out family living and farming activities. Lincoln State Park - Crawford School site (unmarked), nature center, a lake and facilities for boating, swimming, camping, hiking, picnicking.

Abraham Lincoln lived a quarter of his life in Indiana, having moved there with his parents in the autumn of 1816, when he was seven years old. Years later, Lincoln recalled that his father came to Indiana "chiefly on account of the difficulty in land titles in K[entuck]y" and "partly on account of slavery." The Land Ordinance of 1785 subdivided Indiana neatly into sections by government survey, and the Northwest Ordinance of 1787 outlawed slavery there. The Lincolns settled near Little Pigeon Creek in western Perry (now Spencer) County.

At first, Lincoln's mother, Nancy Hanks Lincoln, cared for her family in a rough shelter called a half-faced camp. By early 1817, a sturdy log cabin housed the family. Autumn frosts of

1818 had already colored the foliage of the huge oak, hickory, and walnut trees when Nancy Lincoln became desperately ill, stricken with milk sickness, a poisoning caused by the white snakeroot plant. Cows ate this abundant weed, passed the poison on in their milk, and people who drank this milk or ate its products faced death. On October 5, 1818, Nancy Hanks Lincoln died. She was taken to her final resting place overlooking the Indiana farm she so dearly loved.

Lincoln's New Salem State Historic Site
   R.R. 1, Box 244A
   Petersburg, Illinois 62675
   (217) 632-4000   www.lincolnnewsalem.com

This site features a restored 1830s frontier village, including shops, Rutledge Tavern (where Abraham Lincoln worked and lived), self-guided tours, campgrounds, showers, toilets, picnicking, gifts, refreshments, rest rooms. Administered by the State of Illinois Preservation Agency.

In March 1830, Thomas Lincoln gave up his 100-acre farm at Little Pigeon Creek, Indiana, to move westward to Macon County, Illinois. Spurred by stories of the fertile Illinois soil, combined with a fear of the "milk sickness" which claimed the life of his first wife, Nancy, Thomas Lincoln sold his Indiana

property. He settled on a plot of land north of the Sangamon River and tried to raise corn, but his sojourn to this area was brief. In March 1831, Thomas Lincoln moved on to Coles County, Illinois.

By this time, Thomas Lincoln's son, Abraham, had grown to young adulthood. At age 22, he decided to make his own way in the world. Today, a commemorative stone marker indicates Abraham Lincoln's first home in Illinois. Nearby is a memorial cabin representing the original home, the last that Thomas Lincoln and his son lived in together. The site, until recently called the Lincoln Trail Homestead State Park, is now closed to the public.

Shortly after Abraham Lincoln left his father he met Denton Offutt, who hired him to take his goods by flatboat from Springfield to New Orleans. An unexpected delay, caused by a mill-dam, forced Lincoln and Offutt to stay temporarily in the small settlement of New Salem. Offutt decided that it would be profitable to set up a store there. He hired Abraham Lincoln to run it, thus giving Lincoln his first exposure to merchandising. Abraham Lincoln stayed in New Salem for six years (1831-37), working at a number of jobs, including postmaster and store operator.

Today, all of the buildings of the original New Salem site are reproductions, except Onstot Cooper's Shop. In 1839 (two years after Lincoln left) the county seat was moved to nearby Petersburg. As commercial activity increased at the new county seat, it declined in New Salem, leading to the village's demise. In the early 1900s, an organization known as the Old Salem Chautauqua Association aroused interest in reconstructing the old village. In 1906, newspaper publisher William Randolph Hearst agreed to purchase the site and convey it in trust to the Association. In 1919 the Association conveyed the property to the state of Illinois. In 1932, reconstruction began through the combined efforts of private contractors for the state and the Civilian Conservation Corps. The cooper's shop had already been restored to its original site in 1922. Authentic 1830s furnishings were collected for use in the reconstructed homes. Today, guides dressed in period costume explain what life was like in New Salem.

Lincoln Home National Historic Site
   413 South 8th Street
   Springfield, Illinois 62701-1905
   (217) 492-4241 – Ext. 22   www.hps.gove/liho

Features: The house, a Visitor Center with a bookstore, orientation film, exhibits and rest rooms. Other Lincoln sites, located nearby, include the Old State Capitol State Historic Site, where Abraham Lincoln gave his "House Divided" address; the Lincoln Herndon Law Offices State Historic Site; and the Great Western Depot, where Abraham Lincoln delivered his Farewell Address to the people of Springfield in 1861. Administered by the National Park Service.

When a young state legislator named Abraham Lincoln first came to Springfield, Illinois, in 1837, the town was a relatively small community with a population of about 3,000. Springfield was, in many respects, like a farming village. Its streets

were still unpaved and pigs, cows, and horses wandered about. In this town, Abraham Lincoln made his final transition from frontiersman to lawyer and statesman. While living in Springfield, he drew upon the education that he had begun "by littles," as he described it. He had spent much of his time in New Salem, Illinois, studying law and pursuing a political career. In Springfield, both of these careers blossomed, thanks to Lincoln's innate skills with the English language and the network of friends and associates he established. He acquired a reputation as one of the best trial lawyers in the state, successfully arguing some major cases in which the decisions became landmarks. Here he also met and married Mary Todd, a member of a wealthy and influential family.

Abraham and Mary Todd Lincoln began their married life in 1842, living in the Globe Tavern in Springfield, paying rent of $4 a week. After their first son, Robert Todd Lincoln, was born, they realized that they would need a larger, more prominent place to live.

Reverend Charles Dresser of St. Paul's Episcopal Church in Springfield owned a home on the corner of 8th and Jackson Streets. He had been trying to sell the house since 1841, as he wanted a larger home himself. Lincoln bought the home on January 16, 1844, by paying $1,200 in cash and by surrendering title to a lot he owned worth $300. Thus Abraham Lincoln acquired the only home he ever owned.

The house, originally constructed in 1839 for Rev. Dresser, was a one-and-a-half story, Greek-revival style home built four feet above street level and reached by a set of wooden stairs. Painted white with green shutters, it included a kitchen, dining room, and two large front rooms. The frame of the house consisted of rough-sawn oak, the siding was made of walnut, and the plaster lath was hickory. The house was assembled using handmade nails and wooden pegs. The stairway to the second floor is made of walnut and still survives today.

In 1987-88, the National Park Service, which currently administers the property, completed a two-year restoration program designed to reinforce the structure of the home. It has been open to the public since 1887 and, in recent times, visitation can exceed 1,000 visitors a day. In a previous restoration, a climate control system was installed to protect the furnishings on exhibit. A significant portion of the structural material of the house is original, and the furnishings were either owned by the Lincolns or were made around the time the Lincolns lived in the home.

On February 6, 1861, President-elect Lincoln and his wife held a farewell reception in their home. On February 8, the Lincoln family vacated their home and moved into a Springfield hotel. On the morning of February 11, Abraham Lincoln delivered his Farewell Address and left Springfield with his son, Robert Todd Lincoln. The following day, Mrs. Lincoln left with her two other sons, and joined Lincoln in Indianapolis.

Lincoln Cottage a/k/a Anderson Cottage
U.S. Soldiers' & Airmen's Home
3700 North Capitol Street, N.W.
Washington, D.C. 20317
(800) 422-9988

Please call the site to arrange a visit. Administered by the National Trust for Historic Preservation.

Located on the grounds of the U.S. Soldiers' & Airmen's Home, Anderson Cottage, as it was once known, served as the summer White House for three presidents in the 19th century. Close to the heart of our nation's capital, yet far cooler than downtown Washington was in the stifling hot and humid summer months, Anderson Cottage was an ideal retreat for the presidents and their families.

Built in 1841, Anderson Cottage was originally the farmhouse of George Riggs, co-founder of Riggs National Bank. It is a Gothic Revival residence with pitched roofs, gingerbread trim and gable ledges. Originally 38-feet wide and 32-feet deep with two stories and a basement, it was later expanded by adding an east and west addition to accommodate Riggs' growing family. Pursuant to legislation passed by Congress in 1851, at the behest of General Winfield Scott, the government purchased the 256-acre Riggs farm, including its farmhouse, for use as a home for retired or disabled soldiers. Assisting in the effort to push the legislation through Congress was Brevet Major Robert Anderson, for whom Anderson Cottage is named. Perhaps to underscore his commitment to the home, originally known as the U.S. Military Asylum, General Scott invited his friend, President James Buchanan, and his secretary of war, to be the first president to occupy Anderson Cottage as a summer White House. Buchanan declined, but took up residence elsewhere on the grounds. Later, President Lincoln became the first president to occupy Anderson Cottage in the summers of 1862 through 1864, and, accordingly, Anderson Cottage is also known as President Lincoln's summer White House.

At Anderson Cottage, President Lincoln prepared the second draft of the Emancipation Proclamation. Also, an assassination attempt occurred in August 1864, while Lincoln was riding alone on his horse not far from the cottage. Hearing a gunshot, the President spurred his horse and rode home unharmed, but lost his hat. Investigating soldiers later recovered the hat, which had a bullet hole through the "stovepipe." Mrs. Lincoln suffered a carriage accident in the summer of 1863 when the coachmen's seat broke and the horses bolted. She was forced to jump out of the carriage and received a blow to the head. She lay incapacitated at Anderson Cottage for three weeks. Finally, Lincoln was observed riding on his horse toward Anderson Cottage on the evening of April 12, 1865, the night before he was assassinated at Ford's Theater.

Andrew Johnson Birthplace
  (Mordecai Historic Park)
  One Mimosa Street
  Raleigh, North Carolina 27604
  (919) 834-4844

The park includes the restored birthplace, the original Mordecai plantation house, and several other examples of 18th and 19th century architecture. It also includes a gift shop and the Ellen Mordecai Herb Garden. Administered by Capitol Area Preservation, Inc.

The small, gambrel-roofed structure, generally recognized as the house in which President Andrew Johnson was born, is jokingly referred to as "the wandering birthplace of Andrew Johnson." It is believed that the birthplace was originally a kitchen building located in the courtyard of Peter Casso's Inn, corner of Fayetteville and Morgan Streets, directly across from the North Carolina State House in Raleigh. Sometime after 1867, the house was moved to 118 East Cabarrus Street, where it was rented. On July 1, 1904, it was sold for $100 to the Wake County Committee of the Colonial Dames of America, which presented it to the city of Raleigh. The city moved the house to two different locations in Pullen Park, across from the campus of North Carolina State University in Raleigh. On July 9, 1975, the house was moved to its present location at Mordecai Historic Park, and was restored and opened to the public two years later.

Andrew Johnson National Historic Site
  Depot and College Streets
  Greeneville, Tennessee 37743
  (423) 638-3551

The site features Andrew Johnson's two Greeneville homes (1830s and 1851), his tailor shop (enclosed in the Visitor Center), and his burial site. Administered by the National Park Service.

In 1826, 17-year old Andrew Johnson and his family moved to Greeneville. He later married Eliza McCardle, and built a successful tailoring business. His prosperity enabled him to purchase the brick house on the corner of College and Depot Streets, now part of the Andrew Johnson National Historic Site, where he and his wife lived from the 1830s to 1851. It is a Federal-style, two-story brick structure with white trim and has an ell with an enclosed walkway along its side. Today, three rooms of this house feature exhibits on the Johnson family genealogy and Johnson's early political career. The bottom floor and basement of the house are open to the public.

In 1851, while a Congressman, Andrew Johnson purchased another home in Greeneville, between Summer and McKee Streets, from James Brennan. Except for his years at the White House (1865-1869), Johnson lived here for the rest of his life. The property sits directly on the street in the Northern Irish tradition. Although built in the Federal style popular in East Tennessee in the 1840s, the house has some Greek Revival features. The doorway, particularly noticeable, is flanked by pilasters housing small sidelights. The dentils of the cornice and the transom are also Greek Revival. However, the house also bears a striking resemblance to Johnson's previous home; it is a Federal red brick house with an ell extending into a half-acre lot. Between 1868 and 1869, a second floor was added to the ell in anticipation of Andrew Johnson's return after his term as president.

Grant Birthplace State Historic Site
  Point Pleasant, Ohio 45153
  (513) 553-4911
    Administered by Historic New Richmond.
Grant Boyhood Home
  219 Grant Avenue
  Georgetown, Ohio 45121
  (937) 378-4222
    Privately owned by Mr. & Mrs. John A. Ruthven.

Grant's Birthplace has a thirty-minute tour of the small cottage. The Boyhood Home has a guided tour of the house.

GRANT BIRTHPLACE.

In 1822 an itinerant tanner, Jesse Root Grant, and his wife, Hanna Simpson Grant, rented a cottage in the quiet hamlet of Point Pleasant, Ohio, on the banks of the Ohio River. The opportunity to work in a nearby tannery had drawn the Grants to this village. Their stay was brief, however, for by 1823 Jesse Grant had saved enough for a tanner of his own in nearby Georgetown, 20 miles east of Point Pleasant. Before leaving for Georgetown, a significant event took place in the small cottage: Hannah Grant gave birth to her first son, Hiram Ulysses Grant, on April 27, 1822.

General Grant's other extant boyhood home is currently owned by Mr. and Mrs. John A. Ruthven, who completed restoration in 1982. It is now listed on the National Register of Historic Places, and has achieved National Historic Landmark status. In addition to the Grant tannery across the street (today a privately owned house), visitors can see the two schoolhouses that Grant attended. The first is on the other side of Grant Avenue and is privately owned; the second is owned by the state of Ohio and is closed for anticipated repairs. Visiting both the birthplace and the boyhood home, one may see how the Grant family prospered through hard work, and how the future general and president, despite his modest beginnings and sporadic formal education, grew to become a West Point graduate, a military hero, and a holder of the highest office in the land.

GRANT BOYHOOD HOME.

Ulysses S. Grant National Historic Site
  "White Haven"
  7400 Grant Road
  St. Louis, Missouri 63123
  (314) 842-3298

White Haven features the Main House, Barn/Visitor Center (information desk), book and gift shop, exhibits, the Chicken House, Ice House and stone building on 9.5 acres. Administered by the National Park Service.

Graduating from West Point in 1843 where, due to a clerical error, Hiram Ulysses Grant became known as Ulysses Simpson Grant, Lieutenant Grant began his long army career by reporting to Jefferson Barracks near St. Louis. After arriving he visited the family of his former West Point roommate, Frederick Dent, at the Dent family home known as "White Haven," an

WHITE HAVEN.

1100-acre plantation located along Gravois Creek. The name appears to originate from the Dent family ancestral home in Maryland, which possibly was named for a region in England. It was at White Haven that Lt. Grant met Frederick Dent's sister, Julia. Spurred by news that his regiment was about to transfer, Lt. Grant proposed to Julia in 1844 and eventually married her in 1848. The engagement was lengthened by Grant's departure from Missouri to participate in the Mexican War. As a wedding gift, Grant's father-in-law, "Colonel" Frederick Dent, presented the newlyweds with 80 acres of White Haven farmland that later came to be known as "Hardscrabble."

Despite the subsequent outbreak of the Civil War, which revived his military career, Grant never lost contact with his White Haven home. Rather, he became increasingly involved. During the war he paid the property taxes on White Haven and in 1865 became sole owner and manager. During his presidency (1869-1877), he had tenants who acted as caretakers, and he wrote very specific instructions on what kinds of crops to plant and how to tend to his farm animals. President Grant's original intention was to retire there after leaving office; he even arranged for a railway line to be extended toward White Haven, which was used by Grant, friends, and others in visiting the plantation in 1873. Circumstances compelled Grant to abandon his plans to retire at White Haven, although he retained ownership of the farm until a few months before his death.

Grant's Farm ("Hardscrabble")
10501 Gravois Road
St. Louis, Missouri 63123
(314) 843-1700   www.grantsfarm.com

Features: General Grant's restored log cabin, a fence built from 2,563 Civil War rifle barrels, the Bauernhof courtyard stables, the Tier Garten (housing various species of animals), and Deer Park (a 160-acre game preserve). Operated by the Anheuser-Busch Companies, Inc.

After a two-year separation from his wife and two children, Grant resigned from the military and returned to St. Louis, reportedly telling a friend, "Whoever hears of me in ten years will hear of a well-to-do old Missouri farmer." He established a farm on the 80-acre property received by his wife as a dowry, and called it Hardscrabble. While building a log cabin home on the site, U.S. Grant and his family stayed at his father-in-law's estate, White Haven, and at "Wish-ton-Wish."

The completed cabin is a one and a half story structure. Grant cut its oak and elm logs himself, and also split its shingles and hauled the stones for its cellar and foundation. He shingled the roof, completed the floors and stairs, and had carpenters work on the white window frames, doors, and sashes. Grant observed the tradition of holding a cabin-raising, a party in which neighbors assist in building the cabin. In three days, the building was constructed from the materials Grant had previously prepared. The neighbors were served hard cider and ginger cakes, but did little to help complete the cabin. Thus, the cabin was largely U.S. Grant's own handiwork.

The ensuing years were difficult for Grant, who by this time had to support a wife, two sons, and a daughter. He found that farming did not earn an income adequate to support his family. It is also possible that he was suffering from malaria during this period.

Today the cabin is the property of the Busch family. Anheuser-Busch officials completely restored the deteriorating cabin in 1977. Furnishings typical of the period were located and an effort was made to restore the cabin as nearly as possible to descriptions of the home as it was in General Grant's time there. Most visitors to the site see only the exterior of the cabin while passing it on a trackless train ride. However, visitors can view the interior of the cabin during Grant's birthday celebration in April, or in early October.

The cabin is a memorial to a man who overcame many setbacks and went on to become both a military hero and holder of the nation's highest office.

U.S. Grant Home State Historical Site
511 Bouthillier Street
Galena, Illinois 61036
(815) 777-3310

The site includes no special features other than the home itself. The park across the road includes picnic tables and a log home with Grant pictorial exhibit. Administered by the Illinois Historic Preservation Agency.

In 1865, General Ulysses S. Grant returned in triumph to Galena, where he had lived prior to re-entering military service at the outbreak of the Civil War. Upon his return, the citizens decided to honor his military triumphs with special gifts. After

a parade through the streets, the Grants were escorted to a beautiful Italianate-bracketed brick mansion sitting high upon a hill overlooking the town. A small group of local Republicans had arranged to purchase this house; records show that the house was purchased by Thomas B. Hughlett of Galena in consideration of $2,500 and that title was subsequently transferred to General Grant. The house had been erected in 1860 as a home for the former city clerk, Alexander J. Jackson.

Although the house remained in Grant's name from 1865 to 1885, he spent relatively little time at this residence. This was largely because of his election to the presidency in 1868, his service in that high office for eight years, and his world tour from 1877 to 1879. During his long absences, a series of caretakers who lived in Galena kept the house in order and ready for General Grant and his family whenever they chose to use it.

Grant Cottage State Historic Site
P.O. Box 990
Saratoga Springs, New York 12866
(518) 587-8277

Features: Cottage, scenic outlook of the Hudson Valley, gift shop. Tour lasts 20 to 30 minutes. Administered by the Friends of Ulysses S. Grant Cottage in cooperation with the New York State Department of Parks

In June 1884, Grant, heavily in debt, decided to write his memoirs. Several months later, in November, while dictating to his secretary, he felt a terrible pain in his throat. The cause of the pain was throat cancer, and the disease eventually claimed his life.

On February 27, 1885, General Grant signed a contract with his friend, Mark Twain, to publish his memoirs. By May 23, Volume I went to press. However, Grant knew that he must finish them in order to provide the income his family would desperately need after his death. To complicate matters, summer was approaching and it would be difficult to concentrate on his writing in the oppressive New York City heat.

Fortunately for the Grant family, Joseph W. Drexel of New York made a cottage available to the Grants. It sat atop Mt. McGregor in Saratoga County, New York. The cottage, which Mr. Drexel had recently purchased, was built by Duncan McGregor, and was located near the 300-room Balmoral Hotel in Wilton, New York. It is a two-story structure surrounded by a covered porch and, today, after a paint analysis, it has been painted in its original color scheme – a gold house with dark green and red trim.

The Grants arrived at the cottage on June 16, 1885. For the next several weeks, General Grant battled the disease and the specter of death in a race against time to finish his memoirs. In July, Mark Twain visited Grant to tell him that advance sales of the memoirs would assure royalties of at least $300,000 for Mrs. Grant and her family. (The memoirs eventually earned $450,000 in royalties.)

General Grant finished his memoirs on July 19, 1885. On July 23, four days after the task was completed in its entirety, the eighteenth president of the United States died of throat cancer.

Today, visitors touring the cottage where General Grant died see it furnished just as it was on that day. The furnishings were arranged by order of Mr. Drexel to accommodate Grant and his family. The first room visitors see is the room that was used by Grant's secretary as an office during his stay here. Today it contains a gift shop and a small exhibit.

In another room adjoining the former office, the so-called "sick room," visitors see the two chairs on which General Grant spent most of his time. His fans, candle and lamp are also in this room. A portion of his wardrobe is here, as well as a large case containing medical appliances that he and his physicians used at the cottage. A smaller case holds his pencil and pads, two messages to friends, and the pen he used to do his last writing.

Rutherford B. Hayes Presidential Center
Spiegel Grove
Fremont, Ohio 43420-2796
(419) 332-2081   www.rbhayes.org

The center includes the residence, Presidential library, museum, 25-acre wooded estate, tomb of President and Mrs. Hayes, trees named for prominent guests, video presentation. Affiliated with the Ohio Historical Society.

The nineteenth president of the United States, Rutherford B. Hayes was born on October 4, 1822, in Delaware, Ohio. Like his predecessor, Andrew Jackson, Hayes was born after the death of his father. He was the fifth child of Rutherford Hayes, Jr. and Sophia Birchard Hayes, but he and his sister, Fanny Arabella Hayes, were the only two children who survived into adulthood. Hayes' parents, of Scottish descent, had made the 43-day journey by wagon from Dummerston, Vermont, to Ohio in 1817. The house in which President Hayes may have been born was said to be the first brick house in Delaware, Ohio. A two-story structure with a wooden addition, it was located on the corner of William and Winter Streets. It was torn down in the 1930s to make way for a gasoline station, despite an attempt to save the building.

In 1850, Hayes became reacquainted with Lucy Webb, whom he had met in 1847 while visiting his birthplace in Delaware. A native of Chillicothe, Ohio, she graduated from Cincinnati Wesleyan Women's College in June 1850. On December 30, 1852, Rutherford Hayes and Lucy Webb were married. They first lived with Mrs. Hayes' mother at 141 West Sixth Street in Cincinnati. In 1854, they moved to 383 Sixth Street in Cincinnati, a narrow three-story house. Neither of the houses on Sixth Street exists today. By this time, their first child, Birchard Austin Hayes, had been born, and was later followed by seven other children.

In May 1873, Mr. Hayes returned to Fremont (Lower Sandusky had been renamed, and Hayes had played a role in its renaming shortly before leaving for Cincinnati), to make his uncle's home at Spiegel Grove his permanent home. Spiegel Grove was named by Hayes' uncle, Sardis Birchard, because after a rainstorm, pools of clear water on the grounds reflect its grove of trees like mirrors ("spiegel" is the German word for mirror). As early as November 5, 1845, intending to establish a home to pass on to his nephew, Sardis Birchard had acquired the property from the heirs of Jacques Hulburd, one of the first settlers in the area. Building of the residence at Spiegel Grove began in 1859 and D.L. June, a prominent local contractor, was hired for the job. Sardis Birchard had his wish as his nephew, Rutherford Hayes, and his family, moved to Spiegel Grove.

Upon his arrival, Rutherford Hayes, given free rein to do as he wished with the property, set about adding two frame buildings to the grounds. In Hayes' time, these buildings contained a kitchen, office, and library for his large book collection.

Sardis Birchard died in January 1874, and Rutherford Hayes inherited Spiegel Grove. Mr. Hayes attempted to change the name of the estate to "Birchard Grove" in honor of his beloved uncle, but the name did not stick. Spiegel Grove remains the name of the estate to this day.

While still in office, President Hayes began the custom of naming trees in Spiegel Grove in honor of prominent guests. When his old regiment gathered at Spiegel Grove on September 14, 1877, the president named five oaks after five of his visitors. These trees became known as the "Reunion Oaks." Some of the names given to trees at Spiegel Grove include: William McKinley, James A. Garfield, and William Tecumseh Sherman.

In 1889, Lucy Hayes died, and Hayes' remaining few years were lonely. In 1893, he became ill in Cleveland while enroute to Fremont. Although urged to remain in Cleveland, he remarked: "I would rather die at Spiegel Grove than to live anywhere else." He continued on his journey, and died quietly at Spiegel Grove on January 17, 1893. President and Mrs. Hayes are both buried in a tomb on the Spiegel Grove property.

Between 1909 and 1914, the president's family, through Colonel Webb C. Hayes, conveyed Spiegel Grove to the state of Ohio (the first 10 acres were deeded on March 30, 1909). The gift was conditioned on the construction of a fireproof library and museum on the grounds to house the president's papers and effects. Thus, the Hayes library became the first freestanding presidential library. The library is open to the public as a research and reference center without cost. Admission is charged for tours of the house and museum. In 1928, Congress authorized the donation of several iron gates formerly used at the White House to Spiegel Grove. These were installed at various spots on the perimeter of the grounds.

JAMES ABRAM GARFIELD

**James A. Garfield National Historic Site
("Lawnfield")
8095 Mentor Avenue
Mentor, Ohio 44060
(216) 255-8722**

The site includes the home, Visitor Center in an old carriage house, a museum and video presentation. Administered by The Western Reserve Historical Society, which owns the collection on display. The building and grounds are the property of the National Park Service.

The last of the "log cabin" presidents, James A. Garfield was born in Orange Township (now Moreland Hills), Ohio, on November 19, 1831. Garfield's father, an industrious man, had been apprenticed to a farmer, but saved enough money to buy his own farm in Orange Township. When James Garfield was two years old his father died. Raised by his mother on the Cuyahoga County farm, he was pampered because he was the youngest and most intelligent child in the family. In 1848, he worked briefly as a mule driver on the canal, then later as a carpenter in Chester, Ohio. The following year, his mother had saved enough money to send young Garfield to Geauga Seminary in Chester. He later studied at Western Reserve Eclectic Institute (today known as Hiram College) in Hiram, Ohio, and Williams College in Williamstown, Massachusetts. At Williams, he formed a friendship with the college president, Mark Hopkins. He also taught penmanship briefly at an academy in North Pownal, Vermont, (the academy where Garfield's 1880 vice presidential running mate, Chester A. Arthur, was headmaster a few years before Garfield's stint there).

The next period of James Garfield's life was eventful. In 1856, he returned to Ohio to teach at Western Reserve Eclectic Institute, and became its president a year later at age 26. He also became an ordained minister of the Disciples of Christ denomination, thereby becoming the only minister to serve as president of the United States. He studied law, and in 1860 passed the bar examination and was admitted to the Ohio bar. In 1858, he married Lucretia Rudolph, from a well-respected family. During this period, Garfield lived in a two-story white frame house at 6825 Hinsdale Street in Hiram. The house is privately owned today.

In 1876, Garfield purchased a 118-acre farm, and later added another 40 acres. The farmhouse was a dilapidated, one and one-half story structure known as the James Dickey Farm. Garfield enlarged it from nine to 20 rooms to accommodate his wife, five children, and his in-laws.

As president and party leader, one of Garfield's priorities was to heal the rift between the so-called "Stalwart" and "Half-Breed" factions of his party. He had already begun by running on a ticket with Chester Alan Arthur of New York, aligned with the "Stalwart" faction of the Republican Party. The next step was to dispense patronage in a manner that would placate both factions. In this process, a number of federal office seekers, numerous because of the changes of administration in 1881, would be disappointed. Among them was Charles Guiteau, who wanted to become U.S. Consul in Paris, but was denied the position after two meetings with President Garfield. Guiteau appeared at the Baltimore and Potomac Station in Washington, where he knew that the president would be on hand to take a train to New England. Charles Guiteau, armed with a gun, shot President Garfield twice. Reportedly, as he shot the president, the assassin declared, "I am a Stalwart and Arthur is President now."

President Garfield lingered on for over two months after the shooting. Taken first to the White House, in September he was moved to Franklin Cottage in Elberon, New Jersey, in the hope this location would aid his recovery. Garfield's progress reversed, however, due to an infection caused by unsanitized hands and instruments used in an attempt to locate the bullet. President James A. Garfield died in Elberon on September 19, 1881.

The Garfield family returned to the house in Mentor, named "Lawnfield" by a newspaper reporter visiting the house during one of James Garfield's campaign speeches from his front porch in 1880. In 1885, four years after his death, Mrs. Garfield added a wing to the house which includes the third floor bedrooms, a laundry room/kitchen, a Memorial Library, and a vault room for storage of Garfield's papers. Funded with approximately $360,000 in private donations sent by a grieving nation to the family, the Presidential Memorial Library houses President Garfield's book collection.

Chester A. Arthur Historic Site
North Fairfield, Vermont 05455
(802) 828-3051

The site has a replica of the home the Arthur family lived in during Chester Arthur's infancy (not exact replica), picnic tables, comfort stations. Administered by the Vermont Division for Historical Preservation.

Chester Alan Arthur, who spent most of his life in New York state, is generally considered to have been born on October 5, 1829 in North Fairfield, Vermont. However, there is controversy as to the exact date and location of his birth. During the 1880 national campaign, when Arthur was the Republican vice presidential candidate, Arthur P. Hinman tried to prove that he was born outside of the United States, and therefore ineligible under the Constitution to serve as vice president. The controversy continues due to inconsistent information sources. The Arthur family Bible records his year of birth as 1829; and the 1850 Census, completed "as of June 1, 1850," records Chester Arthur's age as 20, meaning that he was born on or before June 1, 1830. However, both an 1880 political biography and President Arthur's tomb indicate 1830 as the year of birth. Accounts concerning President Arthur's birthplace also conflict. Some sources state that he was born in Waterville, Vermont — others that he was born in Dunham, Quebec, Canada. Assuming that President Arthur was born in Fairfield, generally considered to be the case, there is also some uncertainty as to where in Fairfield his birth occurred. Therefore, it may never be known with certainty where President Arthur was born and whether he was, in fact, constitutionally qualified to be president of the United States.

Chester Arthur's father, William Arthur, an Irish-born Baptist minister who had graduated from Belfast College, came to Vermont by way of Canada. Once a Presbyterian and, at the time of his marriage, an Episcopalian, Reverend William Arthur converted to the Baptist faith while attending a revival meeting in Burlington. He moved to the Fairfield area in 1828 with his wife, Malvina Stone Arthur, and four daughters. That year, William Arthur was ordained as a Baptist minister and Fairfield Center was the location of his first church. In 1829, he and his family moved to North Fairfield, and Rev. Arthur became pastor of the Old Brick Church, which today stands a short distance northwest of the Chester Arthur Historic Site. The Old Brick Church is also open to the public and administered by the Vermont Division for Historic Preservation. It is generally thought that Chester Arthur was born during this period, the fifth child and first son of Reverend and Mrs. Arthur.

Later, in New York, Arthur became active in Whig politics. He became a Republican when the party was formed. On October 29, 1859, Chester Arthur married Ellen Lewis ("Nell") Herndon of Fredericksburg, Virginia. They first lived at 34 West 21st Street in New York City, Nell Arthur's home before their marriage, and later had three children. At the outbreak of the Civil War, Arthur became engineer-in-chief, with the rank of brigadier general, on the staff of Governor Morgan of New York in 1860, and later, acting quartermaster general of the Army of New York City.

In 1861 the Arthurs moved to a two-story family hotel near 22nd Street and Broadway, and spent their summer in Long Branch, New Jersey. While living at the hotel, Arthur became inspector general for the Army of the Potomac. When Horatio Seymour became the Democratic governor of New York in December 1863, Arthur lost his position on the Republican governor's staff. He returned to private practice but remained politically active, aligning himself with the so-called "Stalwart" faction of the Republican Party and the New York Republican machine led by U.S. Senator Roscoe Conkling. In 1865, the Arthurs moved to a five-story brownstone row house at 123 Lexington Avenue, where they held musicales and entertained graciously. The flight of stairs leading to the main entrance on the second floor has been removed and, today, the structure is a somewhat dilapidated building housing both commercial space (on the ground floor) and residential space (on the upper floors). With the exception of the White House, this was Mr. Arthur's official residence for the rest of his life.

Upon President Garfield's death on September 19, 1881, Chester Arthur took the oath of office as president privately in New York City, and was publicly inaugurated in Washington on September 22. As president, Chester Arthur was both conservative and conciliatory, and his cabinet included Robert Todd Lincoln as secretary of war. Ironically, President Arthur, who was such a beneficiary of patronage, is regarded as the father of the federal civil service program.

The house commemorating Chester Arthur is not intended to be an exact replica of the original, but is symbolic, because other than an old photograph of the Arthur home, there is no known source which can describe the size and shape of the original house. The replica is unfurnished, and displays pictures relating to President Arthur and his career. The site affords a wonderful view of the mountains, hills and farmland, which comprise the pastoral setting where President Arthur once lived.

Grover Cleveland Birthplace State Historic Site
207 Bloomfield Avenue
Caldwell, New Jersey 07006
(201) 226-1810

Features: House with museum exhibits on two and one-half acre property, picnic table. Parking is along the street in front of the home. Administered by the New Jersey Department of Environmental Protection and Energy, Division of Parks and Forestry.

Grover Cleveland, the only president to serve two non-consecutive terms, was born in Horse Neck (now Caldwell), New Jersey on March 18, 1837. His parents, Reverend and Mrs. Richard C. Cleveland, lived in the Presbyterian Manse, the parsonage of the First Presbyterian Society of Horse Neck. Steven Grover Cleveland was named after Reverend Stephen Grover, the first installed minister of the Society. Rev. Grover had proposed the construction of a church and parsonage in 1793. The church was built while Grover was minister, but it was 1832 when the parsonage was finally completed at a cost of $1,490, a large sum for a house at the time. Two years later, Rev. Cleveland was installed as pastor.

When Grover Cleveland was eighteen, he headed west to seek his fortune. He stopped to visit relatives in Buffalo, where his uncle, Lewis F. Allen, had a farm on Grand Island on the Niagara River, and offered him a job. He decided to accept the offer and live at the farm but, before the year was out, his uncle had arranged for him to clerk at a Buffalo law firm. There Grover Cleveland studied law while earning five dollars a week.

Grover Cleveland remained in Buffalo from 1855 to 1882. He first roomed at the old Southern Hotel in downtown Buffalo, then had a suite of rooms in Weed block at Main and Swan Streets. A bachelor throughout this period, he dined at Salem Restaurant, Gerot's French Restaurant and Tifft House. In 1881, Grover Cleveland ran successfully for mayor of Buffalo as a

reform candidate, and lived up to his campaign image by his veto of many crooked measures sent to him by a corrupt city council. In 1882, Cleveland was elected governor by the largest margin of any gubernatorial candidate up to that time. As governor, Grover Cleveland resided in the Executive Mansion in Albany.

In 1885, having been elected president, Grover Cleveland left Albany for Washington, where he confronted a curious crowd that awaited with interest what the first Democrat to occupy the White House in 24 years would say. President Cleveland spoke confidently and without notes in favor of civil service reform and against corruption. Cleveland carried his reform beliefs into his presidency by vetoing special interest legislation and calling for a reduction in tariffs.

On June 2, 1886, Grover Cleveland became the only president to marry in the White House. The 49-year old president married 21-year old Frances Folsum, daughter of a former law partner. The Clevelands had five children, and their second daughter, Esther, remains to date the only child of a president born in the White House.

President Cleveland's conservative economic stance and his support of the gold standard cost him enough political support to remove any possibility of his renomination. Instead, the Democrats nominated William Jennings Bryan, a "free silver" Democrat, who electrified the 1896 Democratic convention with his famous "Cross of Gold" speech. In the end, the Republicans prevailed in 1896 with their candidate, William McKinley. President Cleveland, who disliked Mr. Bryan's economic platform, was pleased.

After leaving office, Grover Cleveland settled in Princeton, New Jersey. His home was Westland, at 28 Bayard Lane, now 15 Hodge Road. He bought the home for $30,915. Built by Commodore Robert Field Stockton for his daughter, it is a classic Georgian-style structure with a pillared front porch, Palladian windows on the upper level, and four squared off chimneys in the center. It was modeled after Morven (which was, until recently, the New Jersey governor's mansion). Cleveland had the house expanded by adding rooms to the rear of the house. Sometime later, these were separated into another house. The house is now privately owned.

Today, the Grover Cleveland birthplace is a house museum with four rooms on the first floor available for viewing. Sharon Farrell, the caretaker for the birthplace home (she and her family use the upper floor as their residence), conducts the tour, speaking to visitors about the history of the house. It remained a church manse until 1913, when it was opened as a house museum by a private foundation. The State of New Jersey acquired the site in 1934. A visit to the home provides a fascinating look at the life of a president who, as he said in his last words, "tried hard to do right."

The New York State Executive Mansion
138 Eagle Street
Albany, New York 12202
(518) 473-7521

The mansion and grounds may be visited on Thursdays by appointment. Administered by the New York State Office of General Services.

From the time that Samuel J. Tilden became the first New York governor to occupy the Executive Mansion in 1874, the tie between the occupant of that mansion and national politics has been close. Governor Tilden became the Democratic presidential candidate two years later, and was locked in such a tight contest with Republican former Governor Rutherford B. Hayes of Ohio that it took a special commission to settle the election by determining that Hayes was the winner. Of the 28 successors to Governor Tilden who have lived in the New York Executive Mansion, three went on to become president (Grover Cleveland, Theodore Roosevelt and Franklin Roosevelt), three became vice president (Levi P. Morton, Theodore Roosevelt and Nelson A. Rockefeller), and three were nominated for president but not elected (Charles Evans Hughes, Alfred E. Smith and Thomas E. Dewey).

The story of the mansion begins in the 1850s, when Albany businessman Thomas Olcott decided to build a house on the hill bounded by Eagle and Elm Streets. Shortly after it was built, the Robert L. Johnsons acquired it. The Johnsons enlarged the house to the size of a mansion by the 1860s. After Samuel J. Tilden was elected governor in 1874, he rented the Johnson house for approximately $9,000 a year to use as his official residence. Governor Tilden's successor, Governor Lucius Robinson, continued to rent the house on Eagle Street until 1877, when Governor Robinson persuaded the state to purchase it.

By the time Grover Cleveland became governor, some doubts were voiced about the wisdom of the state's action in purchasing the mansion. A Grover Cleveland biographer described it as "not a very imposing house, although there is some attempt at architectural beauty of a rather clumsy sort...." But Governor Cleveland was not particularly affected by these doubts because his occupancy of the mansion only lasted a short time. He was elected governor in 1882, but in November 1884, he was elected president. On January 6, 1885, Grover Cleveland resigned as governor, and moved to a small house on Willett Street, where he lived until his inauguration as president.

In 1899, the second New York Governor to become president, Theodore Roosevelt, moved to the mansion. He brought his entire family here from their home at Sagamore Hill, in Oyster Bay, Long Island. Years after their stay in Albany, Roosevelt's daughter, Alice Roosevelt Longworth, recalled the mansion as "a big, ugly, rather shabby house, larger than any house we had heretofore lived in, hideously furnished." Yet the presence of the Roosevelts must have breathed life into the "gloomy abode," for the Roosevelt boys converted the basement into a menagerie of pets, and installed a gymnasium in the top floor hall, where Governor Roosevelt himself refereed boxing matches for his sons and their friends. Their stay here was a brief two years, however, because in 1900 Governor Roosevelt was elected vice president of the United States on the William McKinley ticket, and then moved to Washington.

In 1915, Governor Charles S. Whitman and his wife began a process of refurbishing the mansion by converting its large veranda into an elegant breakfast room. He also began a tree planting tradition at the mansion by planting a weeping elm in back of the mansion to mark the birth of his son. On April 25, 1958, President Harry S. Truman and Governor Averell Harriman planted a sugar maple outside the mansion in observance of Arbor Day. The grove of New York state apple trees on the grounds was planted by Governor Hugh L. Carey, who also began a new tradition on Arbor Day, 1981, by planting a sugar maple in honor of one of his distinguished predecessors, Governor Alfred E. Smith.

When Governor Franklin Delano Roosevelt occupied the mansion he decided that the mansion should become a gubernatorial museum of sorts. He asked former governors and their families to donate some furnishings or objets d'art used during their stay there. In response, Mrs. Theodore Roosevelt sent an engraving of Christopher Columbus. The daughter of Governor Roswell P. Flower sent a marquetry table, but little else came of this idea. Governor Roosevelt himself, however, converted one of the mansion greenhouses into a swimming pool during his two two-year terms as Governor (1929-1932).

On the night of March 23, 1961, while Nelson A. Rockefeller was governor, a flash fire broke out in the mansion, destroying much valuable and irreplaceable art. Resisting pressure to build a new mansion, Governor Rockefeller decided to restore the old one. During his long administration he made several personal gifts to the mansion and its grounds. He also decorated the mansion with fine works of modern art by Picasso, Klee, Miro, Nevelson and others.

President Benjamin Harrison Home
1230 North Delaware Street
Indianapolis, IN 46202
(317) 631-1898

The site features a guided tour of the home (lasting 45 minutes to one hour); bookstore/gift shop, and rest rooms. The third floor is now used as a museum of the Harrisons' artifacts and rotating exhibits. The home also offers numerous educational programs for elementary and secondary school students. Administered by the President Benjamin Harrison Foundation.

A member of a family that had been politically active for three generations, it is no surprise that Benjamin Harrison followed in the footsteps of his distinguished ancestors. His great-grandfather, Benjamin Harrison V, a signer of the Declaration of Independence, was a three-term governor of Virginia. President Benjamin Harrison was born at the North Bend, Ohio, home of his grandfather, William Henry Harrison (the ninth president of the United States for one month) on August 20, 1833. The "Big House" had sixteen rooms, wainscoting on interior walls, and clapboard siding. The home was destroyed by fire in 1858 while his grandfather's widow still lived there. Shortly after his birth, Harrison's father, John Scott Harrison, an Ohio congressman and the only man in American history to be both son and father of a president, moved his family to "The Point," a brick two-story farmhouse on 600 acres in North Bend. The house deteriorated and was razed in 1959, despite attempts by the local chapter of the Daughters of the American Revolution to save it. At The Point, young Harrison, along with his brothers and sisters, was educated until he turned 14 and was sent to private school to prepare for college. The family could not afford a prestigious New England college, so he was sent to Farmers College in College Hill, Ohio, and later to Miami University in Oxford, Ohio. After graduating in 1852, he lived with a married sister in Cincinnati, paying her $5.00 a week, while studying law. On October 20, 1853, he married Caroline Lavinia Scott, daughter of the president of a girl's school in Oxford, Ohio, and the couple moved to The Point, where Harrison continued his legal studies. Harrison was admitted to the Ohio bar at the age of 21.

In March 1854, Benjamin and Caroline Harrison moved to Indianapolis, Indiana, where they rented the first floor of a two-story frame house on North Pennsylvania Avenue for $7.00 a week. Harrison got his first job as a crier at the federal court and became acquainted with town lawyers. Mrs. Harrison, who was expecting her first child, was ill and weak during her pregnancy. On doctor's orders, she stayed with her family for a time, and during the autumn of 1854, lived at The Point.

In 1855, after the birth of their first child, the Harrisons moved to a one-story frame house, which had three rooms with an open shed for summer cooking and cost them $6.00 a month in rent. That same year, Indianapolis lawyer William Wallace, brother of *Ben Hur* author Lew Wallace, invited Benjamin Harrison into partnership with him. The Harrisons moved again, this time to a two-story house on North New Jersey Street.

In 1867, Benjamin Harrison bought two building lots at 1230 North Delaware Street at auction for $4,200. In 1874, he commissioned architect Herman T. Brandt to build a grand 16-room brick Italianate home on the property at a cost of approximately $28,000. Benjamin and Caroline Harrison designed the home, and construction was completed in 1875. They moved into their new home in 1875 with their 20-year old son, Russell Harrison, and their teenage daughter, Mary Harrison. This was Benjamin Harrison's permanent home until his death in 1901.

Harrison won the presidential election of 1888, and began his term on a cold and rainy day, March 4, 1889. The Harrisons spent their summers in Cape May, New Jersey, while President Harrison was in office. In October 1892, Caroline Scott Harrison, elected the first president general of the Daughters of the American Revolution the previous year, died of tuberculosis. President Harrison left the White House a widower, accepting an invitation to deliver a series of law lectures at Stanford University in 1893-94. He then returned to Indianapolis to practice law.

In 1895, President Harrison had the Delaware Street house completely remodeled, replacing the natural gas lighting of the chandeliers and fireplaces, and the old coal-fed gravity furnace heating system with electricity.

The Saxton McKinley House
331 Market Avenue South
Canton, Ohio 44702-2107
(330) 454-3426

Tours of the house are by reservation only on Wednesdays and Saturdays. Owned by the National Park Service, the Saxton McKinley House houses the National First Ladies' Library and the Stark Community Foundation.

President William McKinley is the only president for whom there is not a single extant private resident, other than the White House, which he once called home. He was born in Niles, Ohio, on January 29, 1843. He was the seventh in a family of nine children born to William and Nancy McKinley, who were of Scots-Irish ancestry. His father owned an iron-making business and his mother was active in the local Methodist church.

The house where he was born was a two-story colonial-style structure with lap siding. The McKinleys remained in Niles, where young William attended school across the street from his home, until he was nine, and the family moved to Poland, Ohio.

The subsequent history of the birthplace is tragic. By 1875, J. Benedict owned the building, and part of it was used as a grocery store. By 1893, the City National Bank had been built on part of the site, and the birthplace was moved to the back of the lot, on Franklin Alley, and used as an undertaker's storage space. After McKinley's election as president in 1896, an effort was made to preserve it. The house was divided in half, and the half in which William McKinley was born was moved to Riverside Park, a resort in Evansville, Ohio. Riverside Park proved to be unprofitable, and closed in 1901. Tenants occupied the house until 1908, when it was vacated. Vandals and souvenir hunters severely damaged the abandoned building. In 1909, Lula Mackey, an attorney and President McKinley admirer, purchased the structure and the other half of the house, still in Franklin Alley and also in poor condition. She moved both halves to her 200-acre estate at Tibbets Corners, rejoined them, and fully restored the house, naming it "McKinley Heights." She filled it with McKinley relics and pictures, and for years it attracted visitors. Lula Mackey Weiss died in 1934. Three years later, a fire, probably set by prowlers, struck the restored birthplace. Most of the relics and pictures were salvaged, but the structure burned to the ground. Today, the McKinley Savings and Loan Association stands on the original birthplace site. Across the street, on a site including the spot where the little white schoolhouse that McKinley attended once stood, is the McKinley National Birthplace Memorial. The City of Niles provided the site of the memorial.

In 1860, McKinley entered Allegheny College in Meadville, Pennsylvania, but left within a year due to poor health. He returned to Poland and taught school; then, in 1861 he became assistant postmaster in Poland. That June, he enlisted as a private in the 23rd Ohio Volunteer Infantry, under Lt. Col. Rutherford B. Hayes, and by March 1865 McKinley was promoted to brevet major. After the war, he studied law in Youngstown, Ohio, then entered Albany Law School in New York state. In March 1867, he was admitted to the Ohio bar, and in 1869, was elected prosecuting attorney for Stark County.

While in the Stark County prosecuting attorney's office, William McKinley married Ida Saxton, daughter of James Saxton, a Canton banker, on January 25, 1871. Ida's grandfather, John, was founder of the town newspaper, *The Canton Repository*. McKinley's father bought the newlyweds a home on Market Avenue North in Canton, where they lived for seven years. It was a marriage marred by tragedy, however, for the McKinley's daughter, Katie, died at the age of three and a half, and their second daughter, Ida, did not quite live to be five months old. Ida McKinley became a lifelong invalid, but her husband never wavered in his devotion to her. His attentiveness to his ailing wife won him the sympathy and respect of the electorate throughout his political career.

McKinley, running for Congress in 1876 with his old commanding officer, Rutherford B. Hayes, at the top of the ticket, was elected. When Congress was not in session, the couple stayed with Ida's father (her mother died in 1873) at Saxton House, where the McKinleys had held their wedding reception.

Later, McKinley established a law office at Saxton House, and it remained there for over twenty years. During his political career, he used Saxton House as a retreat from the pressures of public life. Seated at the rolltop desk in his third floor office, McKinley drafted speeches and legislation, planned campaigns for public office, and discussed policy and politics with his aides.

In 1896, McKinley leased his old Market Avenue North home. He celebrated his silver wedding anniversary there, and used it during his presidential campaign, making his "front porch" speeches there. In 1899, he repurchased the house for $14,500, planning to retire there. He and Ida planned changes for their newly purchased home. He made $3,000 in improvements to the house, including an octagonal gazebo. During this time, he also owned a farm in Columbiana County on what is now U.S. 30, near the Stark-Columbiana County line. Many years later, these farm buildings were used as a Western Frontier Museum owned by Robert Lozier. The McKinley farm remains privately owned today.

Re-elected in 1900, McKinley's second term as president began quietly. In April 1901, he left Washington for a six-week transcontinental tour. His wife became ill and decided to spend the summer in Canton. McKinley left Canton to deliver a speech at the Pan-American Exposition in Buffalo, New York, on September 5. The next day, assassin Leon F. Czolgogz fired two shots at the president. McKinley died eight days later, on September 14, 1901. Mrs. McKinley, who continued to live at the house on Market Avenue North, died on May 26, 1907, a few short months before the McKinley National Memorial was dedicated.

The McKinley home on Market Avenue North was used as a hospital from 1908-1910, and later as a nursing home. The home was moved in 1930, and eventually it was dismantled, piece by piece, and the pieces were stored, with the idea of rebuilding the house. However, the parts became so badly weathered and vandalized that reconstruction became impossible. Mercy Hospital stood on the McKinley home site for a time. Today, the hospital is known as Timken-Mercy Medical Center and is in an entirely new location.

Today, the Saxton McKinley House is owned by the National Park Service, which leases the building to the Stark County Foundation, a civic and cultural organization that uses a portion of the building for office space. As befits the ancestral home of a first lady, there is a First Ladies Library in the building.

Theodore Roosevelt Birthplace National Historic Site
28 East 20th Street
New York, New York 10003
(212) 260-1616

Features: A thirty-minute tour of the house museum, which includes two rooms of Theodore Roosevelt exhibits and a series of period rooms. Administered by the National Park Service.

In 1854, a wealthy businessman named Theodore Roosevelt, Sr., and his bride, Martha Bulloch of Georgia, moved into a brownstone house at 28 East 20th Street purchased by his father, Cornelius van Schaack Roosevelt, as a wedding gift. Built in 1848, the house, a three-story structure, was entered by a Dutch "stoop" over an "English" kitchen basement. In 1865, a fourth floor was added. Cornelius Roosevelt had also purchased and presented to his other son, Robert, the house next door at 26 East 20th Street as a wedding gift to him and his bride. Four years later, on October 27, 1858, at the home of Theodore and Martha "Mittie" Roosevelt, their second child, Theodore Roosevelt, Jr., was born.

Although the Roosevelt family left their house at 28 East 20th Street in 1873 to travel and did not return to live there, ownership remained with the Roosevelt family until 1896. In that year it was sold and used for commercial purposes, and given a bow-shaped cast iron shop front. In 1916 a developer purchased the house and demolished it to make way for a small commercial building.

In 1919 Theodore Roosevelt died, and the Women's Roosevelt Memorial Association was formed. They decided on the reconstruction and furnishing of President Roosevelt's birthplace as a fitting memorial. They raised funds to acquire the birthplace site and the Robert Roosevelt home next door. In 1920, the Association cleared the birthplace site and razed the Robert Roosevelt house to make room for a reference library, museum galleries and offices. The project designer, Mrs. Theodate Pope Riddle, one of the first female architects in America, had the distinction of being a *Lusitania* survivor. Her design was based on the appearance and measurements of Robert Roosevelt's home (identical to the birthplace) before its destruction. Unable to find photographs or written descriptions of the house, Mrs. Riddle turned to Mr. Roosevelt's sisters, Bamie (Mrs. Sheffield Cowles, Sr.) and Corinne (Mrs. Douglas Robinson), as well as the president's second wife, Edith (a frequent visitor to the house as a child) for their recollections and advice. Their memories of the house, from wallpaper patterns to furniture placement, was detailed, and the interior was restored accordingly. Mrs. Riddle and the Association managed to assemble about 40 percent of the home's original furnishings. The reconstructed birthplace was opened to the public on October 27, 1923, the 65th anniversary of Theodore Roosevelt's birth.

In 1963 the site was acquired by the National Park Service, along with the Roosevelt home at Sagamore Hill, but it was not until 1976 that the birthplace replica and its contents were subjected to a systematic survey. Restoration got underway, using photographs of the 1923 restoration, carpet samples tucked away in a small closet for fifty years, and the services of the Birge Paper Company of Buffalo, which had made the wallpaper used in the 1923 restoration. The Park Service engaged a small New York City firm to silkscreen the wallpaper for the parlor (Birge, which could no longer print paper by hand, could not reproduce the 23-color block-printed paper it had made in 1923). The Park Service's Historical Center analyzed paint samples to determine correct colors, and repaired or replaced broken or missing hardware. The furnishings were cleaned, polished, and reupholstered. The overall result is a house with period rooms which resemble as closely as possible those in the original house.

Maltese Cross Cabin
   Theodore Roosevelt National Park
   Medora, North Dakota 58645
   (701) 623-4466

The South Unit of the Park, in which the cabin is located, features a variety of scenic locations and trails. The Medora Visitor Center displays personal items belonging to Theodore Roosevelt, ranching artifacts and natural history displays. A scale model of Theodore Roosevelt's Elkhorn Ranch cabin is on display here, and a 13-minute introductory film is shown on a continuing basis. The center also has a bookstore and rest rooms. The North Unit of the Park also has a Visitor Center. It also has a number of hiking trails. Camping is available at both park units. Administered by the National Park Service.

Having endured the double tragedy of the loss of his wife and mother on the same day, February 14, 1884, Theodore Roosevelt was determined to find a way to overcome his grief. He had visited the Dakota Territory on a hunting trip in September 1883 and was interested in the cattle ranching business. Before returning to New York, he had become partners with Sylvane Ferris (whose brother, Joe, had guided him through the Dakota Badlands) and William Merrifield in the Maltese Cross Ranch, located on the Little Missouri River. Originally owned by Messrs. Hawley and Wadsworth, it was operated by Sylvane Ferris and William Merrifield. He initially invested $14,000 of his inheritance in the venture. After the tragic deaths, Mr. Roosevelt shuttled between New York and the Dakota Territory, finishing his term as a New York state assemblyman and campaigning for James G. Blaine for president in the east, and tending cattle, hunting buffalo and wild animals, and wearing cowboy clothes in the Badlands. Upon completing his term in Albany and fulfilling his political obligations, Roosevelt headed back to the Dakota Territory.

The Maltese Cross cabin, Theodore Roosevelt's home in the Dakota Territory in 1884, was moved from its original location (seven miles south of its present location) in 1904, the year he ran for election as president in his own right. (Elected vice president in 1900, he first attained the presidency upon the assassination of William McKinley in 1901.) It was exhibited in various cities and on the grounds of the state capital in Bismarck, North Dakota. It was completely restored and placed in its present location, north of the Medora Visitor Center at Theodore Roosevelt National Park, by the National Park Service in 1959. Each of its hand-hewn ponderosa pine logs was soaked as part of the restoration process.

Sagamore Hill National Historic Site
   20 Sagamore Hill Road
   Oyster Bay, New York 11771
   (516) 922-4447

Features are the house and grounds, garden, pet cemetery, gift shop, canteen (summer only), beverage and snack machines, Old Orchard Museum (formerly home of General Theodore Roosevelt, Jr., containing exhibits relating to Theodore Roosevelt's political career, family life at Sagamore Hill, and to the lives of his six children, films presented here regularly), rest rooms. Administered by the National Park Service.

Before the death of his first wife, Alice Hathaway Lee, Theodore Roosevelt was planning a new home for his family at Cove Neck, Oyster Bay, Long Island, where he had spent happy summer vacations in his late boyhood spotting birds and shooting small game. The extended Roosevelt family had two homes in New York: 6 West 57th Street, owned by Roosevelt's mother Martha "Mittie" Bulloch Roosevelt, and the home at 55 West 45th Street, a small pleasant brownstone. In 1883 he bought 155 acres of land from Thomas Young for $10,000 cash and a $20,000 20-year mortgage. He kept 95 acres and sold the remainder to relatives. He planned to build a substantial home, and to name it "Leeholm" after his beloved wife. He selected New York architects Lamb and Rich to design it in the Queen Anne style. As envisioned by Roosevelt, it would be a fitting

home for a family of stature – a house of dignity, comfort, and hospitality. It would have permanence, with 20-inch thick foundations and joists, rafters, and roof-boards in proportion. It would have ten open fireplaces, providing enjoyment and heat to supplement the two hot air furnaces in the cellar.

In March 1884, Theodore Roosevelt was ready to sign a contract for the construction of the 22-room house (the North Room was added to the house in 1905). Tragically, however, on St. Valentine's Day, 1884, his mother died. His wife, Alice, died on the same day, two days after giving birth to their only child. His dream of a home on Cove Neck appeared shattered. But Theodore Roosevelt now had a daughter (named Alice, after her mother), and he realized that she needed a home. Therefore, on March 1, 1884, he signed a contract with carpenters John A. Wood and Son of Lawrence, Long Island, for construction of the home at a cost of $16,975.

This splendid house captures the multi-faceted nature of the 26th president, and reveals the life of an active, spirited, and prominent American family. A truly unique home, maintained much as it was in Theodore Roosevelt's day, Sagamore Hill still contains most of its original furniture.

Pine Knot
Albemarle, Virginia

Not yet open to the public.

After becoming president in his "own right" in 1905, having won the 1904 election, Theodore Roosevelt and his family embarked on the first of eight visits to Pine Knot, a small frame cottage surrounded by 15 acres of woodland, located 17 miles south of Charlottesville, Virginia, in Albemarle County. Edith Roosevelt had arranged the purchase of Pine Knot from her friend William Wilmer, as a place for much-needed "rest and repairs." At Pine Knot, Edith Roosevelt was able to sleep late, walk, read and ride, while her husband hunted, sometimes starting at dawn, and the children played. At night the family gathered for reading by the fire or needlework. Every Sunday the family attended services at nearby Christ (Episcopal) Church in Glendower.

Unlike other presidential retreats, Pine Knot was never a "summer or winter White House." President Roosevelt never conducted official business here, and his only guest was the writer John Burroughs, who accompanied the president on his final visit to Pine Knot in 1908. The President was too absorbed by matters of state for the remaining ten months of his administration to make another visit. Upon leaving office, Roosevelt and his family made Sagamore Hill their permanent home.

In 1986, the property was purchased by Theodore Roosevelt IV, who in turn transferred it, with the financial assistance of John Kluge of Morven Farms, to the Theodore Roosevelt Association. At this writing, the Association, along with the Pine Knot Advisory Board, an organization consisting of interested Albemarle County and Charlottesville residents, is planning to convert Pine Knot into a historic site open to the public for tours. The projected date of the opening of the site is approximately five years from the date of this writing. The prospect of opening Pine Knot to the public is exciting in that it would afford visitors insights into the personal and family life of one of the most significant presidents in American history.

William Howard Taft National Historic Site (Birthplace)
2038 Auburn Avenue
Cincinnati, Ohio 45219
(513) 684-3262

Features: House museum with three restored rooms and exhibits concerning William Howard Taft's public career and the Taft family, restrooms, a 30-minute guided tour. Administered by the National Park Service.

William Howard Taft was born into the family of prominent attorney, Alphonso Taft, on September 15, 1857. A native of Townshend, Vermont, Alphonso Taft graduated from Yale College (Yale University) in 1833, and from Yale Law School in 1838. He visited several cities in search of a place to settle and eventually chose Cincinnati. He corresponded with Fanny Phelps of Townshend, and married her on August 29, 1841. The couple had five children, but only two, Charles and Peter, lived to be adults.

In 1851, Alphonso Taft purchased a home for $10,000 on 1.82 acres in Mt. Auburn, a fashionable section of Cincinnati. The advent of public transportation in the 1870s changed the character of the neighborhood from wealthy to less affluent. Mr. Taft greatly improved his 1840s Federal brick home, adding a rear wing to the house later that year. The following year, Fanny Taft died of a respiratory ailment, but Alphonso Taft did not remain a widower for long. In 1853 he married Louise Torrey of Millbury, Massachusetts, who became William Howard Taft's mother. "Willie" was the second of Louise Taft's five children. Her first died in infancy.

On June 19, 1886, William Howard Taft married Helen "Nellie" Herron, daughter of a law partner of Rutherford Hayes, after a long courtship. They had three children. The eldest, Robert Alphonso Taft, became a U.S. senator from Ohio and General Dwight Eisenhower's principal opponent for the 1952 Republican nomination. Daughter Helen excelled in educational pursuits, and their youngest, Charles Phelps Taft II, later became mayor of Cincinnati. The William Howard Tafts established a home at 1763 E. McMillan Street in Cincinnati. Nellie Taft's father gave them a lot and Mr. Taft drew on $2,500 of savings and financial aid from his father for the $6,000 cost of the three-story home, located not far from Taft's birthplace. They called their new home "The Quarry." In the 1890s the Tafts rented and eventually sold this home, and today it is a private residence.

Because it was considered inappropriate for a sitting president to vacation outside the United States (Theodore Roosevelt had been the first president to go outside U.S. territorial limits while in office), the Tafts summered at Beverly, Massachusetts, while President Taft was in office.

William Howard Taft left the White House in 1913 and returned to his alma mater, Yale, as a law professor. He was extremely popular with students during his eight years there. He and his family first lived at "Hillcrest," 367 Prospect Street in New Haven, Connecticut – a turreted, "pseudo-Romanesque" mansion. In 1918 and 1919, Taft briefly stayed in Washington at 2029 Connecticut Avenue, while serving as co-chairman of the National War Labor Board. By 1919, the Tafts had moved to 70 Grove Street in New Haven, which has since been destroyed. In 1920, Mr. Taft bought a new home in New Haven at 113 Whitney Avenue for $24,000. In early 1921, he lived at 60 Yale Avenue.

In the 1920 campaign, William Howard Taft supported fellow Ohioan, Senator Warren G. Harding, for president. Harding had delivered Taft's nominating speech at the 1912 Republican Convention. Senator Harding's campaign victory was pleasing to Taft, in part because his friend might make his long-held ambition to be appointed to the Supreme Court a reality. The opportunity arose shortly after Harding's inauguration, when Chief Justice Edward B. White died. President Harding nominated Taft to the post, thus making William Howard Taft's late years the happiest of his life.

Due to heart trouble, William Howard Taft resigned as chief justice in February 1930. On March 8, 1930, he died and was later buried in Arlington National Cemetery. Taft was the only person to serve as both president and chief justice of the United States.

William Howard Taft's birthplace home remained in the family until 1899. In 1961, the Taft Memorial Association, under the leadership of Charles Phelps Taft II, acquired the house and grounds. In 1969, the Association donated the property to the American people. The property was designated as a National Historic Site on December 2, 1969.

Woodrow Wilson Presidential Library (Birthplace)
   24 North Coalter Street (Woodrow Wilson Parkway)
   P.O. Box 24
   Staunton, Virginia
   (540) 885-0897

Features include the historic house (restored to pre-Civil War appearance), a museum with seven galleries covering the life and times of Woodrow Wilson, gardens, rest rooms, gift shop. 30-minute tours include touchable artifacts. The museum is self-guided. Administered by the Woodrow Wilson Birthplace Foundation.

Woodrow Wilson, 28th president of the United States, was born in 1856 in the lovely Shenandoah Valley town of Staunton, Virginia, to very religious parents of Scots-Irish Presbyterian extraction. Wilson was born after his father, Rev. Dr. Joseph Ruggles Wilson, had been called to Staunton to serve as minister of the local Presbyterian congregation. The Wilson family never owned the brick Greek Revival home where they lived from 1855-57. It was a manse owned by the church. The Wilsons were the second ministerial family to live in the house.

Upon arriving at President Wilson's birthplace home, visitors begin the tour at the Woodrow Wilson Museum, which opened in May 1990. The museum includes seven galleries, which trace the life and times of Woodrow Wilson: Family; Princeton; New Jersey; Presidency; War; Peace; and the Garage, which features President Wilson's 1919 Pierce-Arrow limousine. The Museum is self-guided and serves as an introduction to the guided tour of the Manse. Plans are currently underway to construct a new presidential library building on the grounds of the birthplace.

Woodrow Wilson Boyhood Home
   419 Seventh Street
   Augusta, Georgia 30901
   (706) 724-0436

This site features the house and grounds. Open by appointment only. Administered by Historic Augusta, Inc.

The Wilson family left Staunton in 1858, and moved to Augusta, Georgia, where they stayed until 1870. They first lived in a Presbyterian Manse on the north side of the 600 block of Greene Street. The site was razed many years ago. "Tommy" Wilson, who grew up to become President Woodrow Wilson, later moved to a manse located at 419 Seventh Street, near the First Presbyterian Church, with his parents, Rev. Dr. Joseph Ruggles Wilson and Janet ("Jessie") Woodrow Wilson, and two sisters. (His brother was born later.) The manse, a three-story, ten-room dark red brick house with white trim, was built in 1859 and is a restrained Greek Revival style. A Colonial revival porch was added around 1900. The manse, purchased by the church in 1860, is located diagonally across the street from the church at the northwest corner of Seventh and Telfair Streets. This site also includes a carriage house. Next door to Wilson's boyhood home is the boyhood home of Joseph R. Lamar, an Associate Justice of the U. S. Supreme Court, appointed by President Taft. Justice Lamar was a childhood friend of Woodrow Wilson.

In Augusta, "Tommy" Wilson experienced the tragedy of the Civil War firsthand. His father was active in the Confederate cause and his church became a war hospital during this period. (It was also at Augusta's First Presbyterian Church that the convention was held to form the Presbyterian Church in the Confederate States in 1861.) Thus, as a young boy, Woodrow Wilson saw destruction to human life, scarcity of food, and the training and marching of soldiers. This experience helped to form his lifelong aversion to war, and was a key factor in his efforts to keep America out of World War I during his first term in office. "Tommy" Wilson's family remained in Augusta through the beginning of Reconstruction after the Civil War.

The Wilsons moved to Columbia, South Carolina, in 1870. The manse remained church property until 1930, when it was sold into private hands. It was entered into the National Register of Historic Places on February 28, 1979, and has been carefully maintained. Woodrow Wilson's boyhood home in Augusta was sold in 1991 to Historic Augusta, Inc., which has opened the house to the public.

Woodrow Wilson Boyhood Home
1705 Hampton Street
Columbia, South Carolina 29201
(803) 252-1770

Features: Tours of the house and grounds, gift shop, restrooms. Administered by the Historic Columbia Foundation.

In 1870, 14-year old "Tommy" Wilson came with his family to Columbia, where he spent his teenage years. The Wilsons first lived with Mrs. Wilson's brother for two years at the Pryor home, located near the Columbia Theological Seminary (where his father was teaching) at Pickens and Blanding Streets, while their own Columbia home was being built at 1705 Hampton Street. The home on Hampton Street is the only house that Rev. and Mrs. Wilson ever owned. It was built expressly for the Wilsons and completed in 1872. Wilson's mother, Jessie, was happy with the home. Here, Wilson saw people struggling to survive the rebuilding necessary to make Columbia a beautiful southern town once again. He later wrote of his experience and how it affected his decisions as president.

The home is a Tuscan Villa-style structure of the Victorian era; however, because there are fewer gingerbread carvings than on other Victorian homes, it is considered a modest example of Victorian architecture. It is painted a natural gray color and has large bay windows. It has cement front steps, but its original steps were wooden. Coal heated the house when the Wilsons lived there, and gaslight was used for illumination, but the lamps were only lit for a short time each night. It was one of the first homes in Columbia that was fitted for gas jets. It is air conditioned today to maintain a constant temperature for the antique furniture. Many of the furnishings are period pieces donated by the citizens of Columbia. The property is enclosed with a white picket fence, and its gardens were restored by the Columbia Garden Club. The gazebo in the front lawn was made before 1872.

The interior of the home underwent restoration in 1992 and today, visitors are able to tour rooms on the first and second floors of the home, which look much as they did when the Wilsons lived here.

Woodrow Wilson House
2340 S Street, N.W.
Washington, D.C. 20008
(202) 387-4062

Features include a 40-minute guided tour of house, conference room, 25-minute film presentation on Wilson's last days, exhibits, gift shop, rest rooms. Administered by the National Trust for Historic Preservation.

In 1920, while still president, Woodrow Wilson decided to make the nation's capital his home for his post-presidential years (and remains the only former president to have done so). As a surprise for his wife, he purchased a house in the Embassy Row section of Washington. A five-story, red brick Georgian Revival townhouse, designed in 1915 by Waddy B. Wood for the Henry Parker Fairbanks family, its facade features an arch with Doric pillars of gray stone and black iron grillwork over its entrance, and three neo-Palladian windows on its second floor. Edith Wilson, who had watched carefully over him after his 1919 stroke left him semi-paralyzed, continued to do so after he left office. She read to him in their second floor library, where they watched silent films on a graphoscope, and took motor trips in their 1919 Pierce-Arrow limousine through Rock Creek Park and into the Virginia countryside. After living in this house for almost four years, Woodrow Wilson died here on February 3, 1924.

Warren G. Harding Home
380 Mt. Vernon Avenue
Marion, Ohio 43302
(614) 387-9630

Features are the home, grounds, and gardens. Building at rear of home, which served as a press office in the 1920 presidential campaign, is now a museum and gift shop, which includes rest rooms. Administered by the Ohio Historical Society. The Harding Memorial, where the President and Mrs. Harding are interred, is also in Marion.

The 29th president of the United States, Warren Gamaliel Harding, was born in a small saltbox clapboard cottage on today's Rt. 97 in the small, north-central Ohio town of Blooming Grove on November 2, 1865. The cottage was torn down in 1896, but the site has a historical marker and a small stone marker on the southwest corner of the actual location. Harding was the first of eight children born to George Tyron and Phoebe Dickerson Harding. George and Pheobe were Baptists, and Warren Harding was raised in that denomination although his mother converted to the Seventh Day Adventist Church while the Hardings lived in Caledonia, Ohio. In 1867, George Harding finished building his next home on the site of his ancestor's cabin; the cottage was too small for the growing family once their second child was born. Warren Harding's second home, which still stands, is a white two-story frame house with a covered front porch and a rear lean-to addition located 0.6 miles west of Route 288 on Route 97.

On July 8, 1891, at age twenty-five, Warren Harding married Florence Kling DeWolfe, daughter of the richest man in Marion. The new Mrs. Harding, deserted by her first husband, was left with a small child and no support. They were married in a home they had built for themselves at 380 Mt. Vernon Avenue in Marion, and they resided there the entire time they spent in Marion. The site is in excellent condition, and its grounds are attractively kept.

The Harding presidency ended tragically. In 1922, President Harding learned of a scandal in the Veteran's Bureau, which had sold war surplus materials far below value to favored purchasers without competitive bidding, and had also bought new materials well above cost. He allowed Bureau head, Charles R. Forbes, once an intimate of Harding's, to leave for Europe in January 1923. Then came the suicide of Charles R. Cramer, Bureau counsel, who had bought from Harding the home he lived in while a senator. To make matters worse, the Republicans had fared badly in the 1922 congressional elections, attributed to the economic recession after World War I. Worried that the results were a vote of no confidence in his administration, Harding undertook what he called a "voyage of understanding," to take his case to the people and strengthen his popularity. He left on June 20, 1923, and was met in Kansas City by Mrs. Albert Fall, wife of the former Secretary of the Interior, who had resigned several months earlier. The speculation is that Mrs. Fall told him about her husband's role in opening up to private oil companies two huge oil fields reserved by the government for naval use, one located in Elk Hills in California and the other at Teapot Dome in Wyoming, in exchange for bribes. Mr. Fall was convicted of bribery in 1929, but no evidence exists linking President Harding with either the "Teapot Dome" scandal or the Veteran's Bureau scandal. However, these revelations, and others, apparently affected the president, who muttered comments about friends who had betrayed him by the time he reached Alaska.

On July 27, in Seattle, the president was stricken with what his doctor, Surgeon General Charles E. Sawyer, at first diagnosed as indigestion. Later it was suspected that he had a heart attack. By the time Harding arrived in San Francisco on July 29, he seemed to be recovering. Then he was stricken with pneumonia. Attended by a team of distinguished physicians, he again appeared to be recovering. Finally, on August 2, he died in bed while being read to by his wife. Doctors speculated that his death was caused by a blood clot in the brain, but Mrs. Harding would not permit them to perform an autopsy. A funeral train carried the president's body across a mourning nation to his home in Marion, where it was buried in a temporary tomb at Marion Cemetery. Mrs. Harding returned to Marion, staying at the home of Dr. Sawyer due to her kidney ailment. She died in Marion the following year and, upon her death, the Harding house on Mt. Vernon Avenue was deeded to the Harding Memorial Association.

In 1926, President and Mrs. Harding were re-interred in the newly constructed Harding Memorial in Marion, near their Mt. Vernon Avenue home. The Memorial, which cost $786,000, is currently undergoing a four-year renovation at a cost of over $1,200,000 in state and federal funds. At the dedication ceremony in1931, President Herbert Hoover, who had served in Harding's cabinet, said, "Warren Harding had a dim realization that he had been betrayed by a few of the men whom he had believed were his devoted friends. That was the tragedy of Warren Harding."

COLOR IMAGES OF SELECTED HOMES

George Washington's home at Mount Vernon, Virginia.

The birthplaces of President John Adams (right background) and John Quincy Adams (left foreground) in Quincy, Massachusetts. These two homes are located within 75 feet of each other.

The site for Monticello, taken from the Italian word meaning "little mountain," was chosen by Thomas Jefferson himself. Mr. Jefferson designed the house in the formal classical style exemplified by the sixteenth century Italian architect Andrea Palladio.

Thomas Jefferson's Poplar Forest, Forest, Virginia. This octagonally shaped home served as a retreat for President Jefferson and is situated on land he inherited from his late wife's estate.

The above engraving is entitled "Montpelier, Late Residence of Madison." It is an engraving by unknown artist, c. 1836, depicting the home of President James Madison and First Lady Dolley Madison. At this writing, Montpelier, a National Trust for Historic Preservation property, is undergoing restoration to achieve the appearance depicted in the engraving, that is, to its appearance at the time that President and Mrs. Madison were in residence at Montpelier.

The Hermitage: Home of President Andrew Jackson, Nashville, TN

A Greek revival style mansion featuring six Corinthian columns on its front portico, The Hermitage was accessible to President Jackson's visitors via a guitar-shaped carriageway leading to the front entrance.

Lincoln home in Springfield, Illinois.

The Lincoln Cottage, also known as Anderson Cottage and Corn Rigs. This cottage served as the vacation home of several nineteenth century presidents, notably Abraham Lincoln. President Chester Arthur was the last President to use this cottage as a vacation residence.

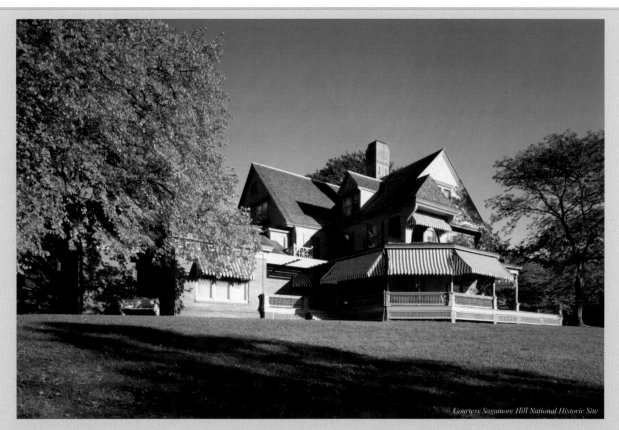

Sagamore Hill, Oyster Bay, New York, home of President Theodore Roosevelt.

This is the birthplace of President Woodrow Wilson in Staunton, Virginia (rear elevation). Today, the birthplace is part of the Woodrow Wilson Presidential Library.

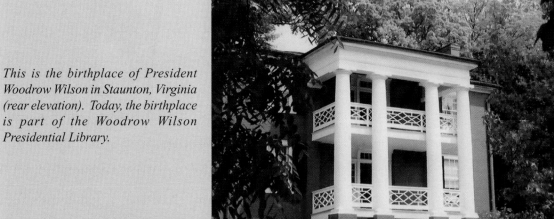

Roosevelt Campobello International Park Commission

Franklin Delano Roosevelt summer home on Campobello Island, New Brunswick, Canada.

© Historic Tours of America, Inc.

The "Little White House" in Key West, Florida, summer home of President Harry S Truman.

The birthplace of President John F. Kennedy in Brookline, Massachusetts.

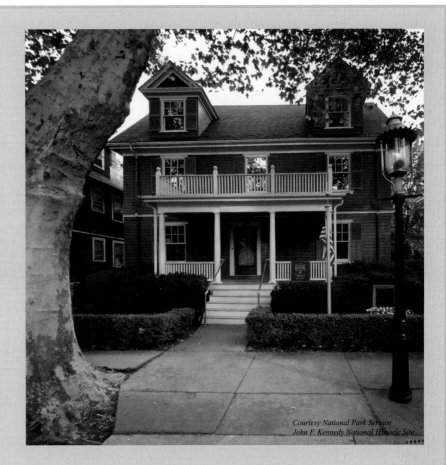

Ronald Reagan boyhood home in Dixon, Illinois. The Reagan family lived here for seventeen years.

President Clinton's first home, where he resided with his maternal grandparents until the age of four, is a two and one-half American Foursquare style home built in 1917. It has been restored and furnished to resemble as closely as possible its appearance during Mr. Clinton's formative years.

An architect's rendering of the Bush Childhood Home in Midland, Texas. The one-time home of President George Herbert Walker Bush and his son, President George Walker Bush, is undergoing restoration at this writing.

CALVIN COOLIDGE

**The Plymouth Notch Historic District
(President Calvin Coolidge Birthplace)
Plymouth Notch, Vermont 05056
(802) 672-3773**

Features include a self-guided tour of ten buildings (staff is stationed in main buildings to assist), Aldrich House (originally President Coolidge's stepmother's house), two walking trails, Visitor Center, museum, restaurant, gift shop, cheese factory, post office, rest rooms. Administered by the Vermont Division for Historic Preservation.

In the small, hilltop community of Plymouth Notch, Vermont, Calvin Coolidge was born on July 4, 1872. His birthplace was a modest, one and a half-story frame structure attached to the town's general store, owned by his father John Coolidge. To the left of the entrance door is the room where he was born. It still includes the bed in which he was born and, like the rest of the cottage, contains original Coolidge family furnishings.

The tour of the Coolidge house includes the sitting room, or "oath of office room," where in the early morning of August 3, 1923, John Coolidge, in his capacity as a notary public, administered the presidential oath of office to his son, an event unique in American history.

While Plymouth Notch was Calvin Coolidge's true home, his long career took him to many residences. In 1905, he rented a home for $28 a month at 21 Massasoit Street in Northampton, which was his official residence until 1930. When he became

governor of Massachusetts, his rent was raised to $40 a month. The house, furnished in an austere fashion, is a simply designed duplex with a front porch and three bedrooms. The front porch was Coolidge's favorite sitting place. Ever frugal, the Coolidges bought linens and silverware from a local hotel after it closed, and did not hesitate to display the insignia. Governmental duties had Coolidge commuting to Boston, where he stayed in a room at the Adams Hotel. After he became lieutenant governor he rented two rooms for his wife and himself. The house on Massasoit Street, now privately owned, was maintained as one of the Coolidge's residences while he was vice president and president, and he returned to the house upon leaving office.

Today, the Calvin Coolidge Birthplace, general store and Homestead are part of a historic district owned and operated by the state of Vermont, Division for Historic Preservation. Among the features of this village is the Plymouth Cheese Factory, reopened by the president's son, John Coolidge, in 1960. On July 4, 1972, the 100th anniversary of Calvin Coolidge's birth, a visitors center was formally opened by the state of Vermont in his memory. It includes a museum store, a sitting room containing portraits of the president and his family, displays of presidential gifts from around the world, and another room featuring a photograph exhibit with text taken from Coolidge's autobiography.

Three additional buildings were recently added to the historic tour: Coolidge Hall, used by the president as his 1924 Summer White House office, a 1927 tourist cabin (which, according to local tradition, was used by the president's chauffeur and secret service), and Aldrich House.

The Beeches
Monroe Street
Northampton, Massachusetts

Privately owned – Home of Bruce and Rita Bleiman

In 1930, the Coolidges moved to "The Beeches," bought for $45,000 from Smith College President Dr. Henry Noble MacCracken in an effort to achieve more privacy. This house, President Coolidge's home for six years until his death on January 5, 1933, is a shingle-sided house with twelve rooms and includes a tennis court and swimming pool. Rear sleeping porches overlook the meadows and the Connecticut River. "The Beeches" is beautifully maintained by its current owners, Dr. Bruce Bleiman and his wife, Rita. The design is influenced by the Queen Anne style. Located in a wooded area in Northampton, it affords a magnificent view of Mount Tom. It includes seven bedrooms, a library from which the former president delivered his radio addresses, two studies, a formal dining room, and a number of asymmetrical small windows. Built in 1915, the home also features a number of innovations for its time, including one of the earliest concrete foundations in Northampton, which contains a basement of nooks and crannies, a small freight elevator (now a linen closet for an upstairs bedroom), electric lights and coal forced-air heat. To avert plaster cracking, the original owner had the downstairs ceilings adhered with canvas throughout. The plethora of windows allow much light into the house, which radiates a cheerful, warm feeling evidencing the Bleimans' tireless, and successful, efforts to maintain an atmosphere of beauty and comfort.

Herbert Hoover National Historic Site (Birthplace)
P.O. Box 607
West Branch, Iowa 52358
(319) 643-2541

Features the birthplace cottage, grave site, the Herbert Hoover Presidential Library-Museum, blacksmith shop, schoolhouse, Friends meeting house, other period houses, Visitor Center, book store, gift shop, picnic shelters, rest rooms. 75 acres of restored native tall grass prairie. Administered by the National Park Service.

In 1874, West Branch, Iowa, was a small settlement on the west branch of the Wapsinonoc Creek, populated mostly by people who had recently migrated from Ohio. Among the inhabitants were a young blacksmith, Jesse Clark Hoover, and his wife, Holda Randall Minthorn. They had a child named Theodore ("Tad") in January 1871, and on August 10, 1874, a second son was born. This boy, born into humble circumstances in the small Quaker community, was destined to serve much of his 90 years of life in the service of others. His name was Herbert Clark Hoover.

The house where Hoover was born is a small, fourteen by twenty feet board-and-batten structure, on the corner of Downey and Penn Streets. The lot on which the cottage stood was purchased for $90 on March 12, 1870. After the birth of their third child, Mary, in 1876, the cottage was cramped, but the family remained there until 1879. Hoover's father and grandfather, Eli, built the cottage in 1871, making some of the furnishings with their own hands. In the small bedroom located in the left-front portion of the cottage, visitors find a small wooden cradle. As the children grew older, they slept in a trundle bed stored under the parents' bed in the small bedroom. Each of the Hoover children used the high chair.

Today, the neighborhood Hoover knew as a child has been preserved and restored by the National Park Service. Visitors can take a self-guided tour of a replica of Jesse Hoover's blacksmith shop, as well as the restored one-room schoolhouse and the Friends Meeting House where the Hoover family worshipped. The birthplace cottage is the original cottage in which Hoover was born, and it has been preserved in a condition that replicates its appearance in the year 1874. Mrs. Hoover had restored the cottage, and the Herbert Hoover Birthplace Society was formed in 1939 for the purpose of managing and maintaining the cottage as a memorial. Today, it is part of the Herbert Hoover National Historic Site. The Herbert Hoover Presidential Library-Museum, operated by the National Archives and Records Administration, is a short distance from the birthplace. Each year during "Hooverfest" weekend, a memorial ceremony is held at President Hoover's gravesite with some of his descendents attending

The Hoover-Minthorn House
115 South River Street
Newberg, Oregon 97132
(503) 538-6629

Features: home, 30-minute tour. No rest rooms. Site sells one book, The Homes of the Hoovers. *Administered by the National Society of the Colonial Dames of America in the State of Oregon.*

In 1883, Herbert Hoover was orphaned. In 1885, at the age of eleven, he moved west to live with an aunt and uncle, Laura Minthorn and Dr. Henry John Minthorn, in Newberg, Oregon, at their invitation. The Minthorns had recently lost a son, and they thought that having another boy in the house might ease their grief. Hoover spent four of his formative years in Newberg, which was a dry, Quaker town at the time.

Lou Henry Hoover House
c/o Stanford University
623 Mirada Avenue
Stanford, California 94305
(415) 723-3419

Features: Home and property on the campus of Stanford University. Administered by Stanford University.

In 1917 the Hoovers commissioned San Francisco architect, Louis Mulgardt, to design their new home. Shortly after engaging him, the Hoovers had an unpleasant surprise – Mulgardt had made his contract with the Hoovers public and the national news services publicized their plans. Given the nation's economic situation, the Hoovers felt that the news was ill-timed. Moreover, they felt that Mulgardt's plans for the house were too pretentious. They decided to dismiss Mr. Mulgardt, paying him for his services up to that date.

This unfortunate episode delayed their plans for the new home. Their intentions to build were revived in early 1919, and the foundation was laid on June 19, 1919. The plans for the house again became public when Hoover was accused by a political foe of building a "palatial residence." In response, Hoover issued a press release stating that the home contained "seven rooms and a basement, a kitchen and a garage." He maintained that the "estate" was only seven rooms on one acre. Hoover did not count the servants' quarters and guestrooms on the other floor, built at a cost of $137,000. Still, the house, while elegant, is not "palatial" in appearance. Mrs. Hoover wanted the house to blend with others in the community.

The Hoovers had selected a vacant lot on San Juan Hill, overlooking the Stanford campus, where, as students, they once sat and enjoyed the view. They leased the land from the university, and selected new architects: Arthur B. Clark, head of Stanford's Art Department, and his son, Birge. Arthur Clark agreed to serve as general supervisor and consultant, but much of the planning effort fell to Birge Clark.

The design and planning of the house was important to Lou Henry Hoover. Herbert Hoover, involved in public matters in Washington and Europe, left the details of the project to her. As reflected in her correspondence with Birge Clark, she involved herself in the design of the house down to the smallest details. The result is an eclectic, tasteful style, and while Clark was the architect, the home is a reflection of the taste and influence of Lou Henry Hoover. Regarding the architectural style, an article in the February 1929 *Western Homes and Gardens* states: "At first glance the exterior of this residence suggests the Pueblo influence, but a closer study of the various elevations reveals the true motif, the Algerian, with every roof an outdoor living room, accessible by a staircase...[T]he house...is a mass of piled up blocks with terraces, outer staircases and fireplaces everywhere inviting freedom and comfort. A dignified unpretentiousness prevails." The Hoovers intended to have a house that was livable, useful for entertaining, and fire resistant. With these considerations in mind, it was designed with low walls, wide terraces, and many windows. Although variously labeled Alge-

rian, Pueblo, or early International, the Hoovers "did not want the house to be related to any historical style."

In June 1920, they moved into the new house, which remained their principal home until Mrs. Hoover's death in 1944. The Hoovers, particularly Mrs. Hoover, enjoyed the special amenities of their home. For example, Mrs. Hoover's study is accessible both by the main stairway and by a "secret" winding stairway leading from her dressing room. In front of the desk in that study were three little windows through which she could see the entrance to the house and, if she saw someone coming, she could come down to greet that person or remain "out of the house" at her election. The house has fireplaces in every principal room and one on the terrace for toasting marshmallows. The house had a swimming pool, which was used by the Hoovers for many swimming parties.

The Hoovers' sons, Herbert, Jr. and Allen, also lived in the house, and once used its basement to build a car, powered by a motorcycle engine. The car had to be removed from the basement by a window. Mrs. Hoover enjoyed driving the small car around the Stanford campus.

Beginning in 1921, the Hoovers spent most of their time in Washington. During that time Herbert Jr. lived in the house while studying at Stanford. As secretary of commerce in the Harding and Coolidge administrations, Hoover lived at 2300 S Street, N.W., in Washington, D.C. This home, occupied by the Hoovers from 1921 to 1928, was originally the home of Major Thomas M. Gales, whose realty firm developed the Kalorama Heights section of Washington in 1901 and 1902. That house has been described as "a nineteenth century house trying to become Georgian."

After leaving the presidency in 1933, President Hoover returned to his house on the Stanford campus. Within a few years, the Hoovers spent most of their time in a suite at the Waldorf-Astoria Hotel in New York City, where Hoover remained until his death on October 20, 1964. Following his wife's death in 1944, Hoover presented the house on San Juan Hill as a gift to Stanford University. Hoover stayed in the house for short periods in the 1940s and 1950s, but the Lou Henry Hoover House, as it is now known, became the official residence of Stanford University's presidents, and remains so today. The home was designated a National Historic Landmark on April 29, 1985.

FRANKLIN DELANO ROOSEVELT

Home of Franklin D. Roosevelt
National Historic Site
Route 9
Hyde Park, New York 12538
(914) 229-9115

Features: Home, museum, library, gardens, gravesites of Franklin and Eleanor Roosevelt, restrooms and two gift shops. Administered by the National Parks Service.

The magnificent grounds of the Franklin D. Roosevelt Home command a fine view of the Hudson River Valley, stretching southward toward Poughkeepsie. This panorama continued to draw the 32nd president back to his home throughout his life. Franklin Delano Roosevelt was born here on January 30, 1882, and it was here that he was laid to rest. That he spent as much time as possible at his family home, Springwood, reflects his great love of that home. Because of occasional stays at this home during his presidency, a series of historic events took place here.

Commonly referred to by the name of the town where it is located, Hyde Park, it is actually "Springwood." Built c. 1800, the two-story structure was bought by Roosevelt's father, James, in 1867. Franklin Roosevelt and his mother, Sara Delano Roosevelt, later hired architect Francis W. Hoppin to modernize it, and add wings to the north and south. The stone and stucco alterations were completed by 1916 and the house remains unchanged to this day.

Upon his death on April 12, 1945, in Warm Springs, Georgia, President Roosevelt's body was transported by train to his Hyde Park home and was laid to rest on the grounds three days later. His wife Eleanor and the children surrendered their rights and interests in the house and 33-acre estate, transferring title to the U.S. Department of the Interior on November 21, 1945. On November 10, 1962, Eleanor was laid to rest beside her husband in the Rose Garden, which is surrounded by a 150-year old hemlock hedge. Today, the home and grounds are administered by the National Park Service, which has preserved them as a shrine to the memory of the man who held our nation's highest office longer than any other.

Roosevelt Campobello International Park
459 Route 774
Welshpool, New Brunswick
Canada E5E 1A4
(506) 752-2922   www.fdr.net

Features include a Reception Center, Roosevelt Cottage, James-Sara Roosevelt Cottage site, Prince Cottage, Hubbard Cottage, Wells-Shober Cottage, natural areas (2,800 acres of R.C.I.P. land). Administered by the Roosevelt Campobello International Park Commission.

For natural beauty of its waters and woodlands, no site can surpass the tiny Canadian island off the eastern coast of Maine known as Campobello. The magnificent scenery afforded to visitors who stand on its cliffs looking toward the coast of Maine, facing the Bay of Fundy, has drawn people to this spot since its first settlers arrived 1770. Just over 100 years after its first settlement, a group of wealthy Americans saw the island's potential as a summer resort and developed a cluster of magnificent summer homes, calling them cottages. Among those was

a country gentleman and businessman, James Roosevelt, who purchased a four-acre estate and a partly completed house overlooking Friar Bay in 1883. The Roosevelts spent their first summer on Campobello in 1883, when James came to the island accompanied by his wife, Sara Delano Roosevelt, and their one-year old son, Franklin Delano Roosevelt.

From 1883 to 1921, Roosevelt spent most summers on this tranquil island. Here, he was stricken with infantile paralysis in 1921. He returned to Campobello only three times, and by the first of these visits, in June 1933, he was president of the United States. By this time, Roosevelt had altered his traditional vacation plans to include frequent visits to Warm Springs, Georgia, where he received therapeutic treatment for his polio.

Little White House and Museum
Warm Springs, Georgia 31830
(706) 655-5870

Features include the "Little White House," guest house, servants' quarters/garage, museum, walkway of stones and flags of the states, fountain, gift shop, snack bar, picnic grounds and rest rooms. Administered by the Georgia Department of Natural Resources.

The Little White House is a monument to the indomitable courage of a man stricken with a debilitating disease. In 1921, the year after Roosevelt had suffered his only electoral defeat as Democratic candidate for vice president of the United States, he was stricken with infantile paralysis while vacationing at his beloved Campobello Island. His legs were paralyzed and his political aspirations threatened. With the devotion of his wife, Eleanor Roosevelt, and trusted aide and companion, Louis Howe, he recovered his will and determination, and set out to find a cure for his paralysis and pain.

Shortly after Roosevelt arrived at Warm Springs and bathed in its waters, there was noticeable improvement in his limbs and his disposition. He swam daily and in time, his health improved and he was strengthened by the relaxing, tingling sensation created by the warm water. When his strength had improved sufficiently, he returned to New York, but occasionally traveled to Georgia for treatments at Warm Springs, residing in various summer cottages over the course of his visits.

After his election as president, Franklin D. Roosevelt, never a man to keep his own company or shun the public, continued to join other patients at the Warm Springs Foundation in bathing in the therapeutic waters. He felt a special affinity with all who had come to seek treatment, but especially enjoyed being with the children who came there. He died of a brain hemorrhage while visiting here on April 14, 1945.

Harry S Truman Birthplace State Historic Site
Truman and Eleventh Streets
Lamar, Missouri 64759
(417) 682-2279

Features: Guided tour of house lasting at least fifteen minutes, reception office (sells postcards and books), UAW memorial, tree planted by President Truman's father, flower and vegetable gardens, rest rooms. Administered by the Missouri Department of Natural Resources, Division of State Parks.

Harry S Truman was born on May 8, 1884, in the town of Lamar, Missouri. His father, John Anderson Truman, a mule trader, purchased the home where Truman was born in 1882 at a cost of $685. Despite the fact that it had no electricity, running water, or bathroom, it was an elegant home. Lamar, like many other cities in the area, was still undergoing reconstruction from the Civil War. Streets were paved with gravel and the main square of town had five local bars (or saloons, as they were called). The population of the town was 700 with five people practicing medicine.

The home, built between 1880 and 1881 by a Mr. Blethrode, has six rooms. This early Victorian white frame house was the Truman home from 1882 to March 1885. It stood at the corner of 11th Street and Kentucky Street. Kentucky Street has been renamed Truman Street. Harry Truman's father planted an Austrian pine tree in the yard the day Harry Truman was born, and nailed a mule shoe over the front door to celebrate his son's birth. The tree is still alive today, and is over 100 years old.

Today, the Harry S Truman birthplace is listed in the National Register of Historic Places. The state of Missouri took title to the house in 1957. After visiting the site of President Truman's birth in Lamar, one can see how the simple life depicted here profoundly influenced his life.

The Truman Farm House
12301 Blue Ridge Boulevard
Grandview, Missouri 64030
(816) 254-2720

Features include the Farm Home, old post office used as a garage by Mr. Truman, old chicken house, and various stone markers. Administered by National Park Service.

After leaving Lamar, Missouri, in 1885, Harry S Truman and his family lived in various towns in Missouri, including Harrisonville and Belton. From 1887 to 1890, the Trumans lived at the farmhouse in Grandview owned by his paternal grandparents. In 1890, they moved to the city of Independence, and until 1896 lived in a two-story white frame house at 619 South Crysler Street, which they bought for $4,000. Harry Truman's poor eyesight meant that he had to wear thick-lensed glasses, and could not engage in rough-and-tumble play, so he spent his time reading the Bible, biographies, and history. In 1896, when Truman was twelve, his family moved to 909 West Waldo in Independence, a frame, two-story, gable-front home with large verandas. In 1902, they moved again, to 902 North Liberty Street. The Truman homes in Independence are still standing as private residences, but have been substantially remodeled. In 1900, he got his first taste of politics, working as a page at the 1900 Democratic Convention in Kansas City. He was impressed at hearing presidential nominee William Jennings Bryan speak. In Independence, Harry S Truman met Elizabeth ("Bess") Wallace at a Sunday school gathering. Their friendship, however, was interrupted when his family moved to Kansas City, Missouri.

In 1906, Truman's father asked him to return to Grandview to help run his grandmother's farm. Truman lived in the farm's frame house, located on 600 acres, from 1906-17, helping his father with raising corn, hogs and cattle. This period of his life as a dirt farmer came to an abrupt halt when the United States entered World War I. Harry Truman enlisted, and became a field artillery captain in France. He stayed in the service until 1919.

The National Park Service acquired the site in 1994. Tentative plans are to restore the site to its 1906-1917 appearance.

Harry S Truman National Historic Site
223 N. Main Street
Independence, Missouri 64050-2804
(816) 254-7199

Features: Home, library, Jackson County Courthouse (where 30-minute slide program entitled "Man from Independence" is shown), Missouri Pacific Railroad Station, First Presbyterian Church, Trinity Episcopal Church, Harry S Truman National Historic Landmark District. Ticket/Information Center has 12-minute slide show with narration, showing the inside of the Harry S Truman Home, rest rooms. Administered by the National Park Service.

After World War I, Harry S Truman settled in the home that became his principal residence for the rest of his life. The house at 219 North Delaware Street is striking because of its simple Victorian charm. Its most unique feature, however, is that although the principal residence of a president of the United States until the end of his life, it remained situated in what is still a residential neighborhood.

The house shows few signs of the trappings of office often found in the homes of modern American presidents. The only security precautions taken during the Truman presidency were the installations in 1949 of an iron fence surrounding the property, and a security checkpoint placed in front of the house. A row of large bushes obstructed the view of passersby, insuring the privacy of the president, who frequently enjoyed reading the newspapers on the porch. Mrs. Bess Truman also used the porch when she played card games with her friends.

The original section of the house, which later became the kitchen, was built in 1850. In 1867, George Porterfield Gates, grandfather of Bess Truman, expanded the house in a Victorian style, adding the portions used by the Trumans as a library and dining room. Gates, who commissioned builder John W. Adams

to add an extension at a cost of $8,000, added that main addition to the house in 1887. This extension, facing out onto North Delaware Avenue, includes the current entrance hall and living room.

The Little White House Museum
111 Front Street – Box #6443
Key West, Florida 33041
(302) 294-9911

This site features the House Museum, a 30-minute guided tour (begins every 15 minutes), video, grounds, exhibits on Truman's Presidency and 12 other U.S. Presidents who vacationed here, bookstore and gift shop. Owned by State of Florida and Administered by Historic Tours of America.

Harry Truman first visited Key West in 1946 at the advice of his doctor, Brigadier General Wallace, who ordered him to take a vacation. He stayed seven days and was immediately attracted to the tranquility, quaintness, and the warm tropical climate of the island. The former commandant's residence (base commander's home) at the Key West submarine naval station became the his vacation home. He stayed there eleven times for a total of 175 days. His wife and daughter, Bess and Margaret Truman, accompanied him on four of his stays. His wife regarded the house as a place for boys to get together and play cards, sip bourbon, and fraternize. Truman's vacations were working vacations; his visitors included General Marshall, Dean Atcheson, Clark Clifford, and many world leaders who journeyed to Key West to confer with the president.

The house was renovated and refurbished by the Navy for $35,000 after Truman's election in 1948. Miami interior designer Haygood Lasseter directed the project. The house and furnishings have the airy touch of a summer vacation home. Two pieces of furniture are especially evocative of Harry Truman. A unique poker table, designed and built by the Navy,

can be seen on the enclosed poker porch; the piano was used by the president on his presidential yacht, the U.S.S. *Williamsburg*, berthed at the Navy base while he was in Key West.

The Little White House, built in 1890, is on 2.27 acres of property which was purchased by the Navy in 1854 for $10,400. In 1896, a New York contractor built two frame dwellings for $7,489. In the 20th century, the two frames were joined together into one home for the base commander and served as a temporary home for senior Navy officials until 1945. Thomas Edison stayed there for six months during World War I to finish the development of the depth charge. After Truman left office in 1953, the house reverted to its former use by the Navy as the base commander's home. In 1974, during the waning months of the Nixon administration, the Navy base was closed and supervision of the property was turned over to the General Services Administration. The house, empty and neglected from 1974 to 1986, suffered from vandalism during this period. Vagrants slept in the house and various fixtures were later found to be missing or destroyed.

In 1986, the General Services Administration auctioned the land and buildings at the naval base to real estate developer, Pritam Singh of Massachusetts, for $17 million. He transferred title back to the state of Florida, then leased it. Restoration of the former "Little White House" began in 1989. The restoration team used state archives, historical, and other records to guide them in their efforts to make the home look as it did during the Truman administration. On January 22, 1991, Singh sold his interest and improvements of the Little White House to the Little White House Company, which completed the restoration process. Historic Tours of America, in partnership with the state of Florida, continued the restoration, adding new displays and artifacts. A major effort was undertaken to finish restoring the house to its glory days of the late 1940s and early 1950s.

Visitors to Key West, a lovely enclave of stores, restaurants, and galleries, will experience the sunny climate and restful surroundings that lured President Truman here for so many visits.

DWIGHT DAVID EISENHOWER

Eisenhower Birthplace State Historic Site
208 East Day
Denison, Texas 75020
(903) 465-8908

Features: House, Visitor Center, gift shop, statue of Eisenhower, picnic facilities, rest rooms. Administered by the Texas Parks and Wildlife Department.

David Dwight Eisenhower was born in Denison, a small northern Texas town. His name was later changed to Dwight David Eisenhower because his mother, Ida Elizabeth Stover Eisenhower, was unhappy with "David" as her son's name and did not want him to be called "Dave." He was nicknamed "Ike." Many mistakenly believe that Abilene, Kansas, was Eisenhower's birthplace. Ike himself, when he applied to West Point, listed his birthplace as Tyler, Texas. In fact, he was born in a modest two-story white house on the corner of Lamar and Day Streets in Denison, across from the train tracks on which his father worked. The third of seven sons (one of whom died young) born to David and Elizabeth Eisenhower, he was the only one born in Texas; all of General Eisenhower's brothers were born in Kansas. The Eisenhower family remained close throughout their lives; in fact, Milton Eisenhower, the Eisenhower's youngest son, became an aide and advisor to his brother when he became president.

The birthplace home, a frame house with three gables, was built c. 1880 and is situated on a six and one-half acre site. His parents rented it when Dwight Eisenhower was born on October 14, 1890. The family lived there between November 1888 and the spring of 1891. The furniture now in the house did not belong to the Eisenhowers, but dates from the period they lived in the house. There are no original floors or wallpaper in the house, but similar paper with authentic patterns and floorboards similar to the original are now on display.

Eisenhower Center
200 S.E. Fourth Street
Abilene, Kansas 67410
(785) 263-4751

This site features the Eisenhower boyhood home, Dwight D. Eisenhower Library, Eisenhower Museum, Visitors Center and Place of Meditation. The Visitors Center shows a movie about General Eisenhower's life and work, and contains a gift shop and public rest rooms. The Place of Meditation is the burial site of General and Mrs. Eisenhower and their son, Doud Dwight. Administered by the National Archives and Records Administration.

In 1892, before Dwight Eisenhower was two years old, the Eisenhower family moved back to Kansas from Denison, Texas. They settled in Abilene, where they lived in a small rented house on S.E. Second Street through 1898. Eisenhower's father worked in the Belle Spring Creamery Co. as head mechanic. As soon as Dwight Eisenhower and his five brothers (a sixth brother died in infancy) were old enough, each boy worked in the family garden where vegetables were grown for the dinner table, and, when older, worked at odd jobs. In Dwight Eisenhower's case, he worked in the creamery after school and during school vacations to aid his struggling family.

In November 1898, when Dwight Eisenhower was eight, his family purchased for $1,000 a larger, Victorian house at 201 S.E. Fourth Street at the corner of Chestnut Street. Built in 1887, the home is simple in design and typifies 19th century Kansas family homes. The property also had a large barn. Here, young Dwight Eisenhower grew into adolescence, in a home where prayer and Bible reading were a daily ritual. Eisenhower and three of his brothers shared an upstairs bedroom, which had two full-sized beds. The oldest boy, Arthur, had his own small bedroom upstairs.

Eisenhower National Historic Site
97 Taneytown Road
Gettysburg, Pennsylvania 17325
(717) 338-9114

The site includes the Eisenhower home, barn, guesthouse, and cattle barns. Self-guided walks of the grounds, farm and cattle operation, and the skeet range, are available. The Reception Center houses a bookstore, exhibits, restrooms, and an 11-minute video about Eisenhower. Administered by the National Park Service.

In early 1950, General Dwight D. Eisenhower, with his World War II military command behind him, was president of Columbia University and looking forward to retirement. He and his wife, Mamie, had shared a life of constant relocation from place to place, and they had never, even during his tenure at Columbia, owned a home of their own. Their desire for a quiet life out of the public eye led them to search for a place to establish such a home. The Eisenhowers' good friends, George and Mary Allen, encouraged them to pur-

Eisenhower Center

Eisenhower Farm

chase a 189-acre farm owned by Allen Redding in Gettysburg, Pennsylvania. In 1950, after looking at several farms in the area, they decided to buy the Redding farm. The Eisenhowers planned to use the Allen Redding farmhouse, once remodeled, as their retirement home. When the architects began to remodel the home, however, they made an incredible discovery. The brick walls of the farmhouse was actually a veneer for a 200-year old log cabin supported by timbers which were quickly deteriorating. On Mrs.

Eisenhower's instructions, construction workers tried to save as much of the original farmhouse as possible. They salvaged a two-story brick section of the old house and the fireplace and bake oven from a summer kitchen, which stood nearby. By 1955, a new house was constructed around the remains of the Redding farmhouse under the guidance of the chief architect, Milton Osborne. The new house, a modified Georgian farmhouse, includes eight bedrooms, eight bathrooms, a living room, a formal dining room, an attic studio, and a porch.

JOHN FITZGERALD KENNEDY

John Fitzgerald Kennedy National Historic Site
83 Beals Street
Brookline, Massachusetts 02146
(617) 566-7937

A Park Service ranger conducts a guided tour of the house. The basement serves as a reception area with exhibits, a video presentation and sales center. Administered by the National Park Service.

The descendant of two distinguished families of Irish-American Bostonians, John Fitzgerald Kennedy was born on May 29, 1917, at 83 Beals Street in Brookline, a suburb of Boston. The house in which the 35th President was born, a three-story frame house built in 1909, was purchased by his father, Joseph Patrick Kennedy, in 1914 in anticipation of his marriage to Rose Fitzgerald, daughter of John F. ("Honey Fitz") Fitzgerald, who served two non-consecutive terms as mayor of Boston and also served in the U.S. House of Representatives. Joseph P. Kennedy, the son of a well-to-do East Boston family, graduated from Harvard University in 1912 and went into the business of investments, especially stocks, real estate, and banking. At age 25, one year before his marriage, he became president of the Columbia Trust Company, thus becoming the youngest bank president in America at that time. In 1917, the year of John F. Kennedy's birth, he became assistant general manager of the Fore River Shipyards.

The Kennedys had four children while living on Beals Street: Joseph, Jr. (born at Hull, Massachusetts) in 1915, John in 1917, Rosemary in 1918, and Kathleen in 1920. The young family dined together each evening, prayed together at nearby St. Aidan's Catholic Church, and entertained occasionally. While Joseph Kennedy was at work, Rose set about the business of running the household and raising an active group of children.

In 1921, the growing family moved to a larger home at the corner of Abbottsford and Naples Roads in Brookline. The three-story frame house has a large wraparound porch with columns and dentils, and two brick chimneys. Three more children, Eunice, Patricia and Robert, were born here. (Jean and Edward were born later in Boston.) While here, Joseph Kennedy took steps that led to the considerable family fortune. John and his older brother, Joseph, Jr., first attended The Edward Devotion School, a public school, and then the Lower Noble and Greenough School (which later became the Dexter School), a private, nonsectarian school. Today, the Kennedys' second Brookline house is privately owned.

In 1927, when young John Kennedy was ten, the family moved to Riverdale, a well-to-do section of the Bronx, in New York City. Later, they moved to a palatial home in Bronxville, just outside of New York City in Westchester County. That home was later demolished. The Kennedys also had a residence in Manhattan and a rented villa on the Riviera. After completing sixth grade in the Bronxville public schools, 13-year old Jack Kennedy attended Canterbury School in New Milford, Connecticut, then Choate School in Wallingford, Connecticut. The Kennedys spent their winters in Palm Beach, Florida, and summered at Hyannisport, on Cape Cod, Massachusetts, where they swam, sailed, and played on the beach.

Early on, Joseph Kennedy, Sr. had resolved that his oldest son, Joe Jr., would become president of the United States. When Joe Jr. died, Joseph Kennedy pinned his ambitions on Jack, who had been a sickly, somewhat shy youth, but was now a war hero due to the PT-109 incident. Father and son went to the family winter residence at 1095 Ocean Drive, Palm Beach, to map out young Jack Kennedy's political future. The house is a white stucco structure with a red-tiled roof and six bedrooms, where the Kennedys had spent vacations. That house is now privately owned.

Just before President Kennedy's parents left his birthplace home in 1921, they sold the house to the wife of Edward E. Moore, close friend and business associate (after whom the Kennedys' youngest child, Edward Moore Kennedy, was named). In 1961, the town of Brookline placed a commemorative plaque on the house, and in May 1965, it was designated a National Historic Landmark. The Kennedy family repurchased the house in 1966. Mrs. Rose Kennedy supervised the restoration of the house to its 1917 appearance. In 1967, Congress authorized the inclusion of the house in the National Park System as a National Historic Site.

As visitors tour this house, they get a sense of what life was like for an active, growing American family around the time of the First World War. It is fortunate that Mrs. Rose Kennedy took such an active part in restoring a place where American history was made, and where one can learn of the formative years of a man who grew up to become a renowned and, tragically, martyred world leader.

LYNDON BAINES JOHNSON

Lyndon B. Johnson State Historical Park
Stonewall, Texas 78671
(830) 644-2252
Administered by the Texas Parks and Wildlife Dept.

Lyndon B. Johnson National Historical Park
(LBJ Ranch District)   (Johnson City District)
Stonewall, Texas   Johnson City, Texas
(830) 844-2241   (830) 868-7128
Administered by the National Park Service.

Features: <u>State Park</u> — *Visitor Center, Sauer-Beckmann "Living History Farm" and swimming pool.*
<u>National Park, (Ranch District)</u> — *reconstructed birthplace home, cemetery, LBJ Ranch and home, school.*
<u>(Johnson City District)</u> — *Boyhood home, Visitor Center, Johnson Settlement, exhibit center.*

In 1867, shortly after the Civil War, Sam Ealy Johnson, Sr. brought his new bride, Eliza Bunton Johnson, to settle in his native land near the Pedernales River. This dry, rugged land of low-lying hills stretches west from Austin about 80 miles. It reaches Fredericksburg and is known as the Hill Country of Texas. After Sam E. Johnson, Sr. left his original house and farm in Stonewall, his son, Sam Ealy Johnson, Jr., rented it from his father. Sam Johnson, Jr. had been elected to the Texas state legislature in 1904. On October 20, 1907, he married Rebekah Baines, daughter of a former Texas state legislator. Rebekah Baines Johnson had an education unusual for a woman of her day; she had studied at Baylor Female College and, like her husband, held a teaching degree.

Sam Ealy Johnson, Jr. brought his bride to live in the rented farmhouse where Lyndon Johnson was born on August 27, 1908. It was called a "dog-trot" house because of an open breezeway between the two enclosed sections of the house. Today, visitors see a reconstruction of the open-air birthplace, which replaces its 1889 predecessor. The "new" birthplace home was designed to serve as a guesthouse during the Johnson administration. Nonetheless, it provides an idea of what life was like for young Lyndon Johnson and his family while they lived there.

In 1949, Senator Lyndon Johnson purchased a 250-acre ranch from his widowed aunt in Stonewall. Expanded by subsequent purchases, it came to be known as the LBJ Ranch, and, during Johnson's administration, the Texas White House. The ranch house has been expanded greatly since the purchase of the property. Today, the National Park Service owns about 600 acres of the property, which was donated by the Johnson family.

LYNDON B. JOHNSON NATIONAL HISTORIC PARK (STONEWALL UNIT)

LYNDON B. JOHNSON STATE HISTORIC PARK

*LYNDON B. JOHNSON NATIONAL HISTORIC PARK
(JOHNSON CITY UNIT)*

61

The Richard Nixon Library & Birthplace
18001 Yorba Linda Boulevard
Yorba Linda, California 92686
(714) 993-3393

Features include the restored birthplace home with audio presentation by President Nixon, library, museum, gravesite, gardens, movie theater showing 28-minute film entitled "Never Give Up: Richard Nixon in the Arena," 75-seat amphitheater, reflecting pool, First Lady's Garden, gift shop/bookstore. Administered by The Richard Nixon Library & Birthplace.

Richard Milhous Nixon was, to quote his memoirs, "born in a house that [his] father built." Nixon's father, Frank Nixon, who had a lemon and orange grove on the property, constructed the small one and one-half story, five-room frame house. He purchased the 12-acre property in Yorba Linda in 1911, and built the house in 1912 using materials that cost $800. Richard Nixon was born in his parents' bedroom on the first floor to the left of the front entrance to that house.

Frank Nixon and his wife, Hannah, to whom Richard Nixon referred as "a saint," were Quakers. They instilled a respect for peace and the value of an education in their five sons, and Nixon took these lessons seriously. He studied hard and learned to play six instruments: the piano, violin, organ, clarinet, saxophone and accordion.

In 1922, the Nixon family left Yorba Linda to run a combination gasoline station and grocery store on East Whittier Boulevard between Whittier and LaHabra. Their residence was located above the station/store. Later, they moved to a single-family home at 15844 East Whittier Boulevard, and ran The Nixon Market, located next door. The boys worked at the store when they were not in school. In 1924, Nixon went to Lindsay, California, to live with his aunt and to study piano and violin. He also spent two summers in Prescott, Arizona, while Hannah Nixon attended Richard Nixon's older brother, Harold, who had tuberculosis and later died of the disease at the age of twenty-two. Nixon also had three younger brothers: F. Donald Nixon, who died several years ago; Arthur Nixon, who died of tuberculosis and encephalitis at the age of seven; and Edward Nixon.

President Nixon and his beloved wife, Pat, are buried beside each other at a gravesite located on the grounds of his presidential library.

Richard Nixon's birthplace, a National Historic Landmark, has been restored, and his presidential library, entirely funded by private donations, is also located on the site. Flowers surround the home and a bench is in front of the house for resting visitors. The front door leads into the living room, a cozy room with window seats, a fireplace, and simple wooden furnishings. (While living here, Frank Nixon earned extra money by building fireplaces for neighboring houses.) Almost all of the furnishings on display in the house are original; they were placed in storage or dispersed among family members for many years. The Crown piano on which Richard Nixon learned to play is also in this room, along with his violin and clarinet. In the other corner of the room are bookshelves, which contain books he read as a child, including *Pilgrim's Progress* and the autobiography of Benjamin Franklin. Among the pictures on the wall is a framed collage of photographs of Richard Nixon and his four brothers as young boys. On the shelves in the rear of the room are small blue "everyday" dishes used by the Nixon family.

Adjoining the living room is the bedroom where Richard Nixon was born. Unlike most of the home's other furnishings, his birth bed was not taken out of storage, but was salvaged from a garden, where it was used to hold up snow pea plants. On the bed is a wool blanket marked "Ohio 1837," a family heirloom presented to Frank and Hannah Nixon on their wedding day in 1908. On the wall in this room is a framed fan which was carried by Hannah Nixon on her graduation day. It is said that Richard Nixon framed the photograph and poem dedicated to "Mother," both of which are hanging above the bed.

Also adjoining the living room is Hannah Nixon's sewing room, behind which is a narrow stairwell leading to the small bedroom which the Nixon brothers shared as children. (The stairs and upper floor are not open to the public.) In the rear of the house is the kitchen, which contains an antique coal and oil stove and an icebox, neither of which is original to the house. However, a high chair used by the Nixon children is here.

From the modest, yet dignified origins suggested by this house, Richard Nixon rose to become one of the most influential figures of modern American history.

GERALD RUDOLPH FORD

Gerald R. Ford Birthsite Park
32nd and Woolworth Streets
Omaha, Nebraska 68105
(402) 444-5955

Features: Model of home in which President Ford was born, gardens, roster of names and home states of presidents. Administered by the Omaha Department of Parks and Recreation.

Gerald R. Ford, our 38th president, was born Leslie L. King, Jr. on July 14, 1913, at 3202 Woolworth Avenue in Omaha, Nebraska. He was the son of Dorothy Gardner King and Leslie King, manager of his father's wool trading company. The house, a Queen Anne mansion built in 1893, was owned by Mr. King's father, Charles H. King, who was on a trip to the west at the time of his grandson's birth. His birth, on a 101-degree day, was difficult for Mrs. King, who struggled with weakness, ill health and a troubled marriage. On July 30, 1913, she left Omaha with her newborn child to live with her aunt in Oak Park, just outside Chicago, Illinois. The birthplace mansion was sold in 1916 and, in 1971, was destroyed by fire.

The Kings were divorced in January 1914. Sometime that year, Mrs. King and her young son moved to 457 Lafayette Street, SE in Grand Rapids, Michigan. Today, that home is privately owned. They then moved to 1960 Terrace Avenue, SE (today, Prospect), a one and a half-story frame house with a full size front porch, which is now privately owned. In 1916, the future president's mother met a paint salesman, Gerald Rudolph Ford, whom she soon married. He formally adopted young Leslie, who was renamed Gerald R. Ford, Jr. In 1917, the Fords rented a two-family house at 716 Madison Avenue, SE. The home no longer stands; a recreation center is on the site, which is owned by the Kent County government.

In 1921 or 1922, the Fords moved to 620 Rosewood Avenue, SE, in East Grand Rapids, a two-story frame house, now privately owned. Mr. Ford's paint selling business grew and was successful in the long run, but in 1923, business reverses resulted in foreclosure on the house, and the family moved to 649 Union Avenue, SE, in Grand Rapids. Young Ford, or "Junie," grew into adolescence in this house, a three-story residence with a large front porch and bay window. Active in competitive sports, he joined the Boy Scouts and became an Eagle Scout. In the garage in the rear of the property, he formed a clandestine social club, and played penny-ante poker. By the time he was fourteen, he had three half-brothers: Thomas, Richard, and James. The Fords never told him about his adoption or his natural father. So, it was a surprise to 16-year old Gerald Ford when, one day, a stranger approached him at the sandwich shop across from the high school, where Gerald was working to earn extra money, and said, "Leslie, I'm your father." He confronted his mother and adoptive father, who told him the whole story. While shocked, he understood his parents' motive for not having told him of his adoption and went on with his life. He became a star football player in high school, and was a conscientious student.

In June 1951, Ford, a Congressman by that time, moved his family to 1521 Mount Eagle Place, a two-bedroom ground floor garden apartment at Park Fairfax, Alexandria, Virginia. In March 1955, they built a brick and clapboard house at a cost of $34,000 at 514 Crown View Drive in Alexandria. When Steven and Susan were born, they used the same wicker bassinet, decorated with ruffles and ribbons, that Ford had used as a child. The family added a swimming pool to the backyard, and Ford regularly used it for exercise. This was the family home until Gerald Ford became president in August 1974. In January 1977, the Fords sold the house. In 1968, they also bought a condominium in Vail, Colorado, which was sold in 1979. In 1982, the Ford family moved into a newly constructed winter and summer resort home in Beaver Creek, Colorado.

The site on which Gerald Ford was born is now a lovely park. The house was destroyed by fire in 1971. The Gerald R. Ford Museum in Grand Rapids, Michigan, and the Gerald R. Ford Library, on the University of Michigan in Ann Arbor campus, are open to the public. Visitors learn the story of a man of integrity, who served his country and did much to restore the faith of the American people in their system of government.

Jimmy Carter National Historic Site
P.O. Box 392
Plains, Georgia 31780
(912) 824-3413

Features include the Plains depot (the Visitor Center),
Plains High School, Carter Boyhood Home (not open to
the public) and the Carter Home on Woodlawn Drive (not
open to the public; visitor viewing area). Rest rooms.
Administered by the National Park Service.

Jimmy Carter, first president of the United States from his region of the nation since Zachary Taylor, was also the first president born in a hospital. James Earl Carter, Jr. was born in Wise Hospital on October 1, 1924, in Plains, Georgia. His father, James Earl Carter, Sr., called "Mister Earl," was a farmer and storekeeper. His mother, affectionately and reverently referred to as "Miss Lillian," was a registered nurse at the local hospital and devoted to social causes. The Carters had three other children: Gloria (1926), Ruth (1929), and Billy (1937). For the first few years, the Carters lived at a rented house on South Bond Street, next door to the Smith family, whose eldest daughter, Rosalynn, later became Mrs. Jimmy Carter. At age four, his family moved to a farm three miles west of Plains on Preston Road near a railroad flag stop called Archery. Many crops were raised on this farm: cotton, corn, watermelons, Irish potatoes, sweet potatoes and, of course, peanuts. In a modest clapboard cottage that had no indoor plumbing or electricity until he was thirteen, Jimmy Carter grew up, tending to farm chores and reading in silence at the dining room table, a family custom. Today, this home (Jimmy Carter Boyhood Farm), along with Carter's present home on Woodlawn Drive, the Plains train depot, the nerve center of the Carter presidential campaign, and the Plains High School comprise the Jimmy Carter National Historic Site.

On November 17, 2000, the Jimmy Carter Boyhood Farm was opened to the public as part of the Jimmy Carter National Historic Site. The farmhouse, where Carter lived from the age of four until he went to college, has been interpreted with period furnishings. Six audio stations and outdoor exhibits tell the story of Carter's boyhood during the Depression, his life on the farm and his relationships with his neighbors, particularly those of African-American descent. The home of neighbors Jack and Rachel Clark is being restored to illustrate the difficulties they endured in a time of racial segregation, and how the knowledge of those difficulties influenced Jimmy Carter in his youth. Visitors will also see the nearby Carter family store, restored and interpreted to convey a sense of what would be found in a rural supply store of the period, and a tennis court, a unique feature of a southern rural farm reflecting Earl Carter's fondness for the game.

In 1971, Governor Carter and his family moved into the Governor's Mansion at 391 West Paces Ferry Road, NW, in Atlanta. The mansion, which sits on 18 acres, is of the Greek Revival style, three stories high and 25,000 square feet in size. The residence was completed in 1967.

After he left office, President Carter returned with his family to Plains. He and Mrs. Carter have written books; established the Carter Center, a combined presidential library, museum, and policy institute in Atlanta; and worked with Habitat for Humanity, a project dedicated to building homes for the underprivileged. He also speaks out publicly on significant policy issues, and has traveled to many countries to negotiate peaceful solutions of regional conflicts.

For relaxation, the Carters enjoyed visiting their friends John and Betty Pope (a Carter cousin) at their home at Walnut Mountain, not far from Plains. The area is wooded and is ideal for fishing. The Carters loved the area, and together with the Popes built a log cabin for both couples to enjoy. In 1982, Mrs. Carter selected the site, a wooded area owned by the Popes and located on Turniptown Creek. By 1983, the unpretentious two-story cabin was completed. It has a wood shake roof and hemlock logs with joints filled with styrofoam; metal laths and two coats of cement provide good insulation. It has a small porch, and its rooms are filled with furniture made by President Carter, a skilled woodworker.

Ronald Reagan Birthplace
111 Main Street
Tampico, Illinois 61283
(815) 438-2815

Features: Second floor birthplace apartment, Reagan Museum on first floor, gift shop. Administered by the Tampico Area Historical Society.

In 1906, lured by construction of a new canal near the hamlet of Tampico, Illinois, and its potential to draw business, John Edward (Jack) Reagan and Nelle Wilson Reagan came to Tampico to seek employment. They had met as store clerks in Fulton, Illinois, and married in 1904. Jack found employment as a clerk in the Pitney General Store and they rented a spacious apartment above a bakery, across Main Street from the Pitney Store.

Their first son, John Neil Reagan, was born in 1908. On February 6, 1911, their second son, Ronald Wilson Reagan, was born. Both boys were born in a bedroom just off the parlor, facing Main Street. When Ronald was born, his father remarked that "he makes a lot of noise for a little fat Dutchman." His nickname has been "Dutch" since then. A restaurant, two doors from the birthplace, is named the "Dutch Diner" in Reagan's honor.

When Ronald Reagan was three months old, the family moved to a large house on Glassburn Street, across from the park.

Ronald Reagan Boyhood Home
816 South Hennepin Avenue
Dixon, Illinois 61021
(815) 288-3404 / 288-5176

This site contains the boyhood home, reception center, 8-foot bronze statue of President Reagan, barn, vegetable garden, video presentation on Reagan's life in Dixon, gift shop, rest rooms. Guided tour of home lasts about 30 minutes. Administered by the Ronald Reagan Home Preservation Foundation.

On December 6, 1920, Jack and Nelle Reagan moved with their two sons, Neil ("Moon") Reagan, age 12, and Ronald ("Dutch") Reagan, age 9, from Tampico to Dixon, Illinois, where Jack Reagan managed a shoe store owned by H.C. Pitney. The family moved into a two-story Victorian frame house at 816 South Hennepin Avenue. The house, on a lot originally owned by Father John Dixon, founder of Dixon, was built in 1891.

Money was tight for the Reagan family. Nelle Reagan supplemented the family income by sewing, mending and clothing alterations. Later, she sold apparel in a dress shop. Because of the financial struggles, Reagan learned at an early age to save money; as a child, he hid his pennies under a loose ceramic tile in the hearth in the front parlor. Despite the family money problems, "Dutch" Reagan was an active youngster, and later called his Dixon years "the happiest times of my life."

The California Governor's Mansion
1526 H Street
Sacramento, California 95814
(916) 323-3047

Features: Mansion, reception center, introductory video, souvenir shop, rest rooms. Administered by the California Department of Parks and Recreation.

Becoming governor of California on January 2, 1967, Ronald Reagan moved into the Governor's Mansion with his wife, Nancy, and son, Ron Reagan. He was the 13th governor to occupy the Victorian-style home. The Reagans' stay at the mansion was brief, for, as gracious as the house is, its proximity to the corner of 16th and H Streets in Sacramento, and the increasing street traffic, meant that the noise level and degree of privacy of the mansion was no longer what it had been in earlier times. Fire safety was also a concern. For those reasons, the Reagans moved to 1341 45th Street, an English Tudor-style home in a residential area, which was their Sacramento home for the balance of Reagan's two terms as governor. At this writing, none of his successors as governor have chosen to live in the mansion, now a State Historic Landmark and open to the public for tours.

In 1974, his last year as governor, Reagan purchased "Rancho del Cielo" (Ranch of the Sky) for $527,000, at 3333 Refugio Road in Santa Ynez, California, a 688-acre ranch located at an elevation of 2,300 feet in the Santa Ynez Mountains, near Santa Barbara. The house, a five-room adobe heated by fireplaces, is over 90 years old and is still owned by the Reagans. During his presidency, Reagan used this California retreat to relax and to exercise by horseback riding or tending to ranch chores such as fence mending and rail splitting.

George H. W. Bush Birthplace
173 Adams Street
Milton, Massachusetts 02187

Bush Summer Home/Summer White House
Kennebunkport, Maine

Privately owned. Not open to the public.

George Herbert Walker Bush, the 41st president of the United States, was born in a Victorian mansion on Adams Street in Milton, Massachusetts on June 12, 1924. Interestingly, the elder of the second father and son in American history to become presidents was born on a street which is so named because the family of Presidents John Adams and John Quincy Adams lived on that same street in the "Old House," which is several miles away in Quincy. His father, Prescott Sheldon Bush, Sr., was an executive at U.S. Rubber and a graduate of Yale College. His mother, Dorothy Walker Bush, gave birth to her second son in a makeshift delivery room on the second floor of the mansion, which is privately owned today.

In 1925, when U.S. Rubber relocated its headquarters to New York City, the Bush family moved to the affluent suburb of Greenwich, Connecticut, into an English Tudor-style home there. Young George Bush lived there until age seven, walking a mile to get to school. In 1931, the growing family (the elder Bush has three brothers, Prescott, Jonathan and William; and a sister, Nancy Bush Ellis) moved to an 8-bedroom house on Grove Lane in Greenwich, where young Bush was known to have taken his shotgun to an upstairs window to shoot rats foraging in the trash.

In 1937, 13-year old George H.W. Bush entered Phillips Academy in Andover, Massachusetts, where he was known as "Poppy." There, he lived in what is now an all-female dormitory. Graduating in 1942 (several months after the attack on Pearl Harbor), he enlisted in the Navy on his 18th birthday. He enrolled in flight school and was sent to Chapel Hill, North Carolina, for pre-flight training. In early 1943, he became one of the youngest pilots in the Navy, and was assigned to a bomber squadron. Shot down during a bombing raid on the island of Chichi Jima, he was awarded the Distinguished Flying Cross. He had been hit but managed to find his survival raft and stayed afloat until a U.S. submarine found him. He rejoined his squadron in the Philippines and flew 58 combat missions before being sent home for Christmas of 1944.

On January 6, 1945, George H.W. Bush married Barbara Pierce, who he had met at a Christmas dance three years before. They were engaged before he left for the Pacific. The newlyweds went to Trenton, Michigan, renting rooms from Grace Gargone while Bush trained with the Navy. Before he received another assignment, the Japanese surrendered, and World War II ended in August 1945.

With the war over, George H.W. Bush enrolled at Yale, as had his father, and majored in economics. He joined Skull and Bones, the Yale secret society. Excelling at soccer and baseball, he dreamed of an offer to play baseball professionally, but the offer never came. Their first year in New Haven, George and Barbara Bush rented a small railroad flat next to a mortuary. The next year, Barbara Bush was pregnant with their first child, George Walker Bush. The couple moved to a house in New Haven, where George H.W. Bush refused a doctor's re-

quest to carry his pregnant wife up the stairs, joking that she "was as big as anyone on the Yale football team." In 1946, they moved next door to the Yale president, who, on one occasion when he was expecting an important visitor, asked George H.W. Bush to remove his infant son's diapers from the clothesline.

Graduating from Yale in 1948, George and Barbara Bush, with their son, hopped into their Studebaker and set off for Odessa, Texas, where Bush worked as a trainee with a subsidiary of Dresser Industries. They lived in a duplex in Odessa, on what is now a vacant lot. George Bush learned the oil business and how to get involved in the post-war oil boom. After less than a year in Odessa, they moved to California, where Bush took a series of jobs with Dresser Industries. In 1949, they stayed at what is now the Pierpont Inn in Ventura, California, while Bush worked in sales of oil drilling equipment. They stayed in other hotels along the west coast, and also lived in what is now a run-down building in Compton, California. By this time, they had a daughter, Robin, who died three and a half years later of leukemia. They later had four more children: Jeb, Neil, Marvin and Dorothy.

In 1950, the Bushes returned to Texas, and settled in a house in Midland in 1951. Located on "Easter Egg Row" (named for its brightly painted houses) it cost $7,500, and is now privately owned. The town of Midland plans to acquire the house at 1412 Ohio, for a George W. Bush boyhood house museum. During this time, Bush and his friend, John Overby, formed an independent oil company, the Bush-Overby Oil Development Company, Inc. In 1953, the Bushes moved to a house at 405 E. Maple, across from "the most stylish neighborhood," according to Mrs. Bush.

In 1954, Bush's company merged with another small company to form Zapata Petroleum. The following year, a subsidiary, Zapata Off Shore, was formed to manage the parent company's interests in offshore oil drilling, a new technology at the time. That same year, the Bushes again moved, to a ranch-style house with a two-car garage, which they had built for themselves, at 2703 Sentinel. The house bordered on a group of athletic fields.

Zapata Off Shore became a separate entity in August 1959, and Bush became president of his own oil exploration company. The Bushes moved to Houston, and in 1960 moved to a house where they lived until 1967. It was later razed to make room for five new houses. By 1962, Bush, pursuing new challenges, became politically active. (His father, Prescott Bush, Sr., was U.S. Senator from

Connecticut from 1952-1962.) He became the Harris County Republican Chairman that year, and in two years in the post, he revitalized the Texas GOP and increased its membership. In 1964, he challenged incumbent Democratic Sen. Ralph Yarborough, and was defeated despite an energetic race. In 1966, he ran for U.S. Representative from a new district in Houston, and won. He bought a home in Washington, D.C., today used for Italian diplomats. He also moved his Houston residence to a townhouse, which Mrs. Bush notes was burglarized three times while Congress was in session and the family was away.

In 1969, the Bushes moved to a brick two-story home in Washington. Nixon was president, and Bush was being urged to give up his House seat for another race against Senator Yarborough. Bush agreed to run, but Yarborough was defeated in the Democratic primary by a more conservative newcomer, Lloyd Bentsen. Most voters followed their partisan traditions and elected the Democrat, Bentsen, to the post.

After the election, Nixon nominated Bush as U. S. ambassador to the United Nations. The Bushes moved to the ambassador's official residence in New York. After two years in foreign policy, Nixon called upon Bush again, to serve as chairman of the Republican National Committee. Bush was in this post when Nixon resigned and President Ford succeeded him. President Ford wanted to offer Bush an ambassadorship. The two met, and Bush told Ford that he wanted the opportunity to represent the United States in China. Since the United States did not yet formally recognize the People's Republic of China, there could be no ambassador to that country, so Bush was appointed chief of the U.S. Liaison Office in China. The Bushes lived in Beijing for 13 months, where they studied t'ai chi and entertained guests, with Marx Brothers films and the American moon landing. In 1975, President Ford asked Bush to be director of the Central Intelligence Agency. While in the post, Bush had bullet-proof screens installed at his Washington home. Those screens were still in place when the house was sold in 1977, as were Yale decals on some toilet-seat covers.

In 1981, Vice President Bush sold his Houston home, and took a Houston hotel suite as his legal residence and voting address. (In 1988, local Democrats teased him by renting the suite for a party). His family to the vice president's official residence on the grounds of the Naval Observatory in Washington. The turreted, 11-room house, formerly the base commander's home at the observatory, became the vice president's official residence during the Ford administration, for Nelson Rockefeller. Mrs. Bush quipped that the house rocked as she jogged on her treadmill. When they left in 1989, President-elect Bush noted that they had lived in that house longer than in any other residence in over 40 years of marriage.

While president, George H.W. Bush took frequent working vacations in the Bush summer home at Kennebunkport, Maine. This large summer retreat, on a bluff overlooking the coast of Maine, has been a Bush family retreat since the president's grandfather built it in 1901. While the property is private and not open to the public, visitors to Kennebunkport may view the property from a distance by driving along a coastal road.

Vice President's Residence
Observatory Hill
Washington, D.C.

Not open to the public. Administered by the United States Government.

The one-time official residence of President George Herbert Walker Bush during his years as Vice President (1981-1989), the home, a Queen Anne-style Victorian house, stands on a hill once known as Pretty Prospect. The house was designed by Leon Dessez and was built in 1893 for the Superintendent of the U.S. Naval Observatory. In 1929, the Superintendent's House was redesigned as the official home of the Navy's Chief of Naval Operations and became known as the Admiral's House. In 1974, Congress designated that the home become the official temporary residence of the Vice President of the United States. Although then-Vice President Gerald Ford and Betty

Ford anticipated moving into the home as its first official residents in its new designation, they did not do so due to Mr. Ford's sudden ascendance to the Presidency. However, many of the items selected by Mrs. Ford for the house are still in use today.

Each of the occupants of the residence since 1974, Vice Presidents Nelson Rockefeller, Walter Mondale, Bush, Dan Quayle, Al Gore and Dick Cheney have, together with their families, added their own special contribution to improving the home, including the display of impressive works of art (by Vice Presidents Rockefeller, Mondale, Bush and Gore) and restoration and structural improvements (by then Vice Presidents Bush and Quayle).

While not open to the public, the home serves as a site for many official functions and as the official residence of our nation's vice presidents and their families.

THE BUSH FAMILY IN KENNEBUNKPORT, MAINE.

The Arkansas Governor's Mansion
1800 Center Street
Little Rock, Arkansas 72206
(501) 376-6884

Features: Mansion, state police guardhouse, guesthouse, lawns and gardens. Tour of first level of mansion only. Administered by the State of Arkansas.

William Jefferson "Bill" Clinton, our 42nd president, was born on August 19, 1946, at Julia Chester Hospital in the small, rural community of Hope, Arkansas. Clinton's mother, the former Virginia Cassidy, grew up in Hope and married William Jefferson Blythe III, a salesman from Sherman, Texas. Blythe died in an auto accident in May 1946. He was driving to Hope to rejoin Virginia, who was five months pregnant at the time. Four months later, William Jefferson Blythe IV was born.

In the summer of 1953, Billy Blythe and his family moved to a rented home outside Hot Springs, Arkansas, where his stepfather joined his brother's car dealership. After a few months, the family moved into a permanent home at 1011 Park Avenue, a two-story Tudor-style home, now painted white with green trim, in the northern section of Hot Springs. Today, the house is privately owned.

In 1978, Bill Clinton was elected governor of Arkansas. At age 32, he was the youngest governor of any state in the nation at that time. The Clintons moved into the governor's mansion in Little Rock, and on February 27, 1980, daughter Chelsea was born. Later that year, Clinton campaigned for election to a second two-year term, but lost the re-election bid. Remaining in Little Rock to practice law, the Clintons bought a house at 816 Midland Avenue in the Pulaski Heights section, an eclectic, charming neighborhood high atop a hill west of town. The house was built in 1905, a Victorian style with three bedrooms, a front porch, a lawn and garden, and a carport. The house is comfortable and unpretentious, and is currently owned by the Ray Whittier family.

ARKANSAS GOVERNOR'S MANSION

In 1982, Bill Clinton again won election as governor of Arkansas, and was re-elected every other year through 1990. The home in which Clinton resided while governor is a Georgian colonial mansion, on eight acres formerly used by the Arkansas School for the Blind. Bricks from the school were used in the construction of the mansion, situated in the Quapaw Quarter of Little Rock. It was completed in 1950 at a cost of $197,000. The mansion's first occupants were Governor Sid McMath and his family. The main building is a two-story structure measuring 140 by 60 feet. Two cottages are linked to both sides of the main building by circular brick colonnades pierced with portholes. The west cottage is used by the governor's security force, and the east cottage is maintained for visiting state guests. The property is accessible through an iron filigree gate, beyond which is a circular drive surrounding a tiered iron fountain, a gift from the Governor's Mansion Association, the five-member independent commission that oversees all changes and acquisitions concerning the mansion. Adorning the mansion's front entrance is a colonnade with four columns; the Arkansas State seal is affixed to the top. In the back, a terrace runs the length of the mansion. The patio furniture was manufactured in Arkansas.

The Clinton Center
117 South Hervey Street
Hope, Arkansas 71801
(870) 777-4455

Features: The boyhood home, Visitor Center, gift shop, and the Virginia Clinton Kelley Memorial Garden.

When Virginia Cassidy left Julia Chester Hospital with her newborn son, she took him to the home of her parents, Eldridge and Edith Grisham Cassidy, at 117 South Hervey Street in Hope. A two-story frame structure with a front porch and a dormer on the second floor, it was built in the American "four-square" style shortly after World War I by Charles Garrett, who served in France during the war and modeled the house after one he had admired there. Mr. Garrett and his wife, Irene, had lived in the house before his grandparents purchased it in 1938. From 1946 to 1950, Billy Blythe lived in the house on South Hervey Street, entrusted to his grandparents' care while his mother received training as a nurse-anesthetist at schools in Shreveport and New Orleans, Louisiana. Today the house on South Hervey Street is fully restored and was opened to the public in 1997 as an Arkansas State Historic Site.

In 1950, the year Billy Blythe turned four, his mother married Roger Clinton, owner of a Buick dealership in Hope. The Clintons and young Billy moved to 321 East 113th Street, a modest but charming one-story home with three bedrooms, was one of a series of homes built in 1945 by George Peck, for occupation by returning World War II veterans. The Clintons lived there until 1953. Later, Helen Aldridge, who ran a pet grooming business on the property for many years, owned the house. It was later renovated by another owner, Donna Williams, who added a large awning to the side of the house, and installed new carpeting, but kept its essential character. The house was sold recently to two women, a school teacher and a probation officer, who maintain a sign noting that this charming white home with green trim was the boyhood home of Bill Clinton.

From a toddler, Billy's mother and grandparents instilled in him the value of an education. Thanks to his mother's teaching, he could read, write, and do arithmetic at the age of four. Virginia also pursued an education to become a nurse-anesthetist. Billy learned other lessons as well. At Cassidy Grocery, his grandparents' general store, he observed that, even in an era of racial intolerance, his grandfather treated everyone with respect and, unlike other establishments, everyone entered Cassidy Grocery through the front door. Acquired by the Clinton Birthplace Foundation in 1993, the Cassidy home has been restored to reflect its appearance at the time Billy Blythe lived there. The house conveys the modest, unpretentious lifestyle of an American family in the post-World War II era. On the grounds of the Clinton Center is a garden which includes a memorial to Virginia Clinton Kelley. The Visitors' Center features a "Time Line Room" tracing Clinton's life from Hope to the White House, and a replica of the White House Oval Office rug designed by Kaki Hockersmith of Little Rock. Recently, Takeharu Shiraishi, a Japanese businessman who wanted to express his gratitude to the United States, visited the home and decided to build a replica as a tribute. Located in Okinawa, Japan, it is now complete. After leaving office in January 2001, Clinton and his wife, Hillary Rodham Clinton, who had been elected U.S. Senator from New York in 2000, bought a Dutch colonial-style home at 15 Old House Lane in Chappaqua, Westchester County, New York, as their primary residence. They also purchased a $2.85 million home in Washington, D.C., for use by Senator Clinton whenever Congress is in session. These homes are not open to the public.

THE CLINTON CENTER

GEORGE WALKER BUSH

The son of the 41st President (George Herbert Walker Bush), George Walker Bush was born in New Haven, Connecticut on July 6, 1946. He moved with his parents to Midland, Texas and later to Houston, Texas. He received a bachelor's degree in history from Yale University (also his father's alma mater) in 1968, after which he served as an F-102 fighter pilot in the Texas Air National Guard. The future 43rd President then returned to school and received a Master of Business Administration degree from Harvard University Business School in 1975. George W. Bush then returned to Midland, where he embarked on a career in the oil and energy business. After participating in his father's 1988 presidential campaign, he, along with a group of partners, purchased the Texas Rangers baseball franchise in 1989. The future president then became the managing partner of that franchise. During this period, President Bush resided in Dallas, Texas (see photograph). In 1994, Mr. Bush was elected Governor of Texas, beating then incumbent Governor Ann Richards. Governor Bush set a precedent in 1998 when he became the first Texas governor to be elected to two consecutive four-year terms.

In 2000, Governor Bush defeated many other presidential contenders, including Senator John McCain of Arizona and then American Red Cross president Elizabeth Dole of North Carolina (the wife of former Senate Majority Leader and 1996 Republican presidential candidate Bob Dole, who was later elected Senator from North Carolina in her own right) to become the Republican presidential nominee at the party convention in Philadelphia. As his running mate, Gov. Bush chose former Defense Secretary Dick Cheney (who had also served as White House Chief of Staff under President Ford and as Congressman from Wyoming). In the general election, the Bush/Cheney ticket faced the Democratic team of then Vice President Al Gore and Sen. Joseph Lieberman of Connecticut.

After a hard fought campaign, the results, as of Election Night 2000 and for weeks thereafter, were inconclusive. The one point of agreement of both sides was that the election would be settled by the results of the Florida ballot contest. After weeks of recounting of punch card, military and absentee ballots, as well as disputes as which Florida counties' ballots should or should not be recounted, the contest wound up in court and was appealed all the way to the nation's highest court — the U.S. Supreme Court. The election was ultimately settled by the High Court's decision in the case of Bush v. Gore which, in effect, called the disputed Florida contest in Governor Bush's favor. Shortly after the Supreme Court announced its decision, Vice President Gore conceded the election, paving the way for the inauguration of George W. Bush as the 43rd President on January 20, 2001.

Notable among the events of President Bush's first term were: the war in Iraq, in which American forces, with cooperation from forces from the United Kingdom and other nations, attempted to rout out Saddam Hussein and his Baathist Party followers. Ultimately, Saddam Hussein was captured along with many others involved in his regime. The disastrous terrorist attack on September 11, 2001 was the precursor to this military action as well as the invasion of Afghanistan, the purpose of which was to address the threat of the Al Quaeda terrorist network led by Osama bin Laden, as well as to depose the Taliban regime. On the domestic front, the Bush Administration successfully pressed for the passage of an educational reform measure known as the No Child Left Behind Act.

In 2004, President Bush and Vice President Cheney were returned to office, defeating Senator John Kerry of Massachusetts and John Edwards of North Carolina in another hard-fought contest in which the Republican ticket prevailed with 52% of the largest total vote in American presidential election history.

The Bush family currently own a ranch in Crawford, Texas where they go to vacation from the White House.

THE BUSH HOUSE IN DALLAS, TEXAS

THE BUSH CHILDHOOD HOME IN MIDLAND, TEXAS

THE WHITE HOUSE

1600 Pennsylvania Avenue
Washington, D.C.
(202) 456-7041   (202) 472-3669

Features: White House, President's Park (including trees associated with certain presidents), Rose Garden, Jacqueline Kennedy Garden, and Children's Garden. Visitors tour the ground and first floors of the house; the second and third floors are used by the presidential family and guests and are not open to the public. Tours administered by the National Park Service.

George Washington, the only president who never resided in the White House, was instrumental in choosing its location. On July 16, 1790, Congress passed the Residency Act, empowering Washington to select the location of a newly-designed capital city somewhere along the banks of the Potomac River. Plans for the new "Federal City" were drawn by French engineer Pierre L'Enfant, who designed it on the basis of two focal points: the Capitol and the President's House, symbols of the legislative and executive branches of government. At the suggestion of Thomas Jefferson, then secretary of state, the design for the focal buildings was opened to competition, which was announced on March 14, 1792 by the Commissioners for the District of Columbia. On July 17, 1792, James Hoban, an architect who was born and trained in Ireland, was declared the winner for his design, modeled after country houses of the British Isles. The cornerstone for the house was laid by the Commissioners for the District of Columbia and the Freemasons on October 13, 1792, and Mr. Hoban supervised construction of the new residence of the chief executive.

Construction began in 1793, using bricks fired at three kilns located in a brickyard on what is now the north lawn of the White House. Laborers for the project lived in huts in today's Lafayette Park. Stonemasons recruited from Edinburgh and slaves hired from their owners contributed to the construction effort. Materials included stone from the Aquia Creek quarry in Stafford County, Virginia, used for the foundations and exterior walls; wood from North Carolina and Virginia, used for flooring, doors and frames; and lime for the mortar from the Frederick, Maryland, region. By the end of Washington's two terms as president, the walls of the new residence were in place and its roof was framed.

Construction continued as John Adams assumed office in 1797. Because the District of Columbia was still under construction, Philadelphia remained the United States capital for much of the Adams administration (New York City was the first capital, but it was moved to Philadelphia while Washington was president). From 1797 to 1800, the windows of the new President's House were installed and the interior walls were plastered. On November 1, 1800, President John Adams became the house's first occupant, although construction was not yet complete. On his second night in the President's House, Adams, in a cold and unfinished chamber, wrote to his wife (who had not yet arrived) the following words: "I pray heaven to bestow the best of Blessings on this House and all that shall hereafter inhabit it. May none but honest and wise men ever rule under this roof." These words, now carved on the mantel of the state dining room, are the motto of the White House.

Although John Adams and Abigail Adams were already in residence in late 1800 and early 1801, much work remained to complete the interior. Abigail Adams used the unfinished East Room to hang her wash to dry. Defeated for re-election in 1800, Adams spent just a few short months in the house. His successor, Thomas Jefferson, opened the President's House to all visitors, a practice observed to this day. While he was president, the east and west terraces were built.

President James Madison and his wife Dolley occupied the house in 1809. It became a place of entertainment for Washington society. The Madisons hired architect Benjamin Latrobe to design furniture, and decorate the oval room. Then, the British captured Washington and set fire to the house on August 24, 1814. The Latrobe furniture was destroyed, and nothing remained of the house but exterior sandstone walls and interior brickwork. The Madisons moved outside Washington, then to the second floor of Octagon House on New York Avenue. From

1815 to the end of the Madison administration, they lived in the corner house of "Seven Buildings" on Pennsylvania Avenue. The "Seven Buildings" was the only structure between the White House and Georgetown to survive the 1814 fire.

Supervised by James Hoban, the President's House was rebuilt. It was ready to be occupied by President James Monroe, who stayed the first few months of his term at 2017 I Street.

Other significant changes and events have taken place at the residence in its 200 year history. James Hoban was on hand to supervise construction of the north portico in 1824, and the south portico in 1829, Andrew Jackson's first year as president. Under Jackson, the East Room was furnished and opened for public use, and in 1833 running water and a bathroom were installed. In 1848, under President James K. Polk, gas lighting was installed. The first central heating system was installed in 1853 during Franklin Pierce's administration, and bathrooms and water closets on the second floor were improved. While Pierce was in office, a glass conservatory was planned for the west terrace and was completed in 1857, under James Buchanan. While President Rutherford B. Hayes was in office (1877-1881), the conservatory was expanded with walks and benches added to the interior design, and was connected to the mansion through the state dining room.

The White House has been a place of both celebration and mourning. In 1865, thousands of mourners passed by the coffin of slain President Abraham Lincoln in the East Room. On June 2, 1886, President Grover Cleveland wed Frances Folsom in the Blue Room. Several weddings have been held at the White House, but Cleveland remains the only president to be married there.

Under President Benjamin Harrison, electric lights were added to the mansion in 1891. When Theodore Roosevelt became president in 1901, he changed the official name to the White House. He learned of needed structural repairs and more space for the family and staff. Moreover, the interior was a mixture of styles. Congress appropriated funding to both repair and refurnish the house, and construct new presidential offices. The architectural firm of McKim, Mead, and White began work in June 1902. It replaced the old conservatories with the West Wing, an executive office building. By 1909, when William H. Taft became president, even more space was needed, and the West Wing was enlarged. Among the rooms added was the Oval Office. In 1913, during Woodrow Wilson's term, the first roses of the formal garden, now known as the Rose Garden, were planted just outside the Oval Office.

In 1927, under President Calvin Coolidge, a third floor was added for residential space. Two years later, a fire broke out in the West Wing on Christmas Eve, 1929, and President Herbert Hoover left his dinner table to supervise the removal of papers from the Oval Office. While reconstruction of the West Wing progressed, Hoover first used the Lincoln Study (now the Lincoln Bedroom), then space in the State-War-Navy Building (the Old Executive Office Building), as temporary offices. The West Wing was enlarged again in 1934 under Franklin D. Roosevelt, and during World War II the East Wing and an air raid shelter were built, with a movie theater added in the east terrace. In 1948, President Harry S Truman added a balcony to the south portico, but soon it was learned that the White House had serious structural problems due to weakened interior walls and support beams. The Trumans moved across the street to Blair-Lee House for four years while extensive repairs were made: gutting the interior, digging a new basement, laying a new foundation, and installing a steel framework. Fireproofing was installed (in 1965, Lyndon Johnson added a fire detection system), and in March 1952, Truman gave the first tour of the "new" White House.

Successive administrations have added to the White House collection of historic objects and artistic works. Continuing efforts have been made to maintain and preserve the White House. A recent project, restoration of the exterior walls, required stripping 28 layers of paint and repairing the sandstone walls by expert stone carvers. The fine details of these walls, including carved garlands and roses, are now restored to their original appearance.

Modern visitors to the White House begin their tour at the East Wing entrance. Looking through windows in the ground floor corridor, visitors see the Jacqueline Kennedy Garden; both it and the Rose Garden, located by the West Wing, are used for bill signing and other formal ceremonies. The Jacqueline Kennedy Garden is ordinarily used for receptions and events by the first lady, while the Rose Garden is used for ceremonies by the president. In 1971, the wedding of President Richard Nixon's daughter, Tricia, and Edward Cox took place in the Rose Garden. On the White House grounds are trees planted by presidents, including an American elm planted by John Quincy Adams and a magnolia planted by Andrew Jackson.

Visitors enter the ground floor of the house to view the ceremonial rooms. Through the corridors and hallways of the ground and state floors of the White House hang portraits of the presidents and first ladies. Looking to the right, visitors see the library. Its volumes are entirely written by American authors, and include biographies and works of fiction, history, and science. Federal period furnishings are here, as well as a chandelier that once belonged to the family of James Fenimore Cooper. Portraits painted by Charles Bird King in 1821 and 1822 depict five Indian leaders who visited President Monroe. A Gilbert Stuart portrait of George Washington, c. 1805, hangs over the mantel. The paneling in the library, the vermeil room and the china room is made from the 1817 timbers salvaged from the 1948-52 reconstruction of the White House.

Across the hallway is the vermeil (gilded silver) room, displaying a vermeil collection bequeathed to the White House in 1956 by Margaret Thompson Biddle. Over the mantel hangs *Morning on the Seine*, a gift to the White House in late 1963 by the John F. Kennedy family in his memory. Also in this room is a portrait of Eleanor Roosevelt by Douglas Chandor.

Visitors next come to the china room, set aside by Edith Wilson to display china and glass display cabinets. The portrait of Grace Coolidge in this room was painted in 1924 by Howard Chandler Christy. Mrs. Coolidge posed for the portrait because President Coolidge was too busy with events concerning the Teapot Dome Scandal to keep a scheduled appointment to sit for his portrait. Her red dress in the portrait determined the color scheme for this room, and is carried through by velvet lined china cabinets and an English rug, c. 1850. Two early 19th-century chairs known as "Martha Washington" or "lolling" chairs, flank the fireplace. A painting above the mantel, entitled *View on the Mississippi, Fifty-Seven Miles Below St. Anthony Falls, Minneapolis* was painted by Ferdinand Richard in 1858, the year Minnesota was admitted to the Union.

Proceeding up the hallway, visitors next come to the Diplomatic Reception Room. One of three oval rooms in the residence (others are the Blue Room on the state floor and the Yellow Oval Room on the second floor) it was furnished as a Federal period parlor during Eisenhower's presidency in 1960. At that time, the gold-and-white color scheme of the room was determined and such furnishings as a Pembroke table, sofa, and armchairs in the Hepplewhite style were placed in the room. The sofa is flanked by Sheraton-style card tables and there are also two Sheraton-style settees and two matching chairs attributed to the Slover and Taylor workshop of New York. On the floor is an oval rug in the Aubusson style, specially woven for this room; its border displays the emblems of the 50 states. (Due to wear and tear, the rug has been replaced twice, in 1971 and 1983.) A Regency chandelier was added to the room in 1971, while Nixon was president. This room is used ceremonially by new ambassadors and their families, who enter the room directly through the South Grounds entrance to the White House to present their credentials to the president. President Franklin D. Roosevelt broadcast his famous "fireside chats" on the radio from this room. The wallpaper, called "Scenic America," was first printed in 1834 by Jean Zuber et Cie in Rixheim, Alsace, France. It depicts Niagra Falls, New York Bay, West Point, Boston Harbor, and the Natural Bridge in Virginia.

The next room up the hallway is the Map Room, which was used by President Franklin Roosevelt as a situation room from which to follow the military events of World War II. In 1970, during Nixon's presidency, the room was redecorated in the Chippendale style of the late 18th century, and now serves as a private meeting room for the president and the first lady. It contains several examples of "blockfront" furniture, an American adaptation of the Chippendale in which the central of three vertical panels of a piece of furniture is recessed. A blockfront chest made in Massachusetts c. 1760 and a blockfront slant-top desk from Rhode Island dating from between 1760 and 1765 is in this room. On a Philadelphia Chippendale desk is a medicine chest that belonged to James Madison. Taken from the White House by a British soldier in 1814, it was returned in 1939 by one of his descendants. Three landscape paintings by artists of the Hudson River School hand here: Jasper Cropsey's 1876 *Autumn Landscape on the Hudson River*; William Hart's 1858 *Lake Among the Hills*; and Alvan Fisher's 1854 *Tending Cows and Sheep*. The Persian rug in this room is a colorful Heriz, and the cut-glass chandelier seen here, which features rare star pendants, was made in England c. 1765.

Next, visitors proceed to the state floor, where they first view the East Room, the largest room in the White House, used for ceremonies, receptions, press conferences, and other events requiring much space. Several weddings, including those of Ulysses Grant's daughter Nellie, Theodore Roosevelt's daughter Alice, and Lyndon Johnson's daughter Lynda Bird, were held here. The bodies of seven presidents have lain in state here. The room was originally conceived by Mr. Hoban as a "public audience room," and its 18th-century classical style

appearance today largely reflects the work of the McKim architectural firm during its 1902 restoration of the White House under Theodore Roosevelt. The oak floor of Fontainebleau parquetry is notable, as are the three Bohemian cut-glass chandeliers. The wood paneling on the walls, painted white, includes eight relief insets illustrating Aesop's fables. Delicate plaster decorations adorn the ceiling. In keeping with the gold-and-white color scheme envisioned by Mrs. Theodore Roosevelt, gold damask draperies of French fabric were installed in 1983 during Reagan's presidency. Normally, the room contains little furniture, but one piece on display here is a Steinway grand piano with gilt eagle supports and gilt stenciling by Dunbar Beck. Designed by Eric Gugler, it was given to the White House by the manufacturer in 1938. Also here is a full-length portrait of George Washington, a replica made by Gilbert Stuart of his original "Landsdowne" portrait. Except for a period after the 1814 fire, it has hung in the White House since 1814. Dolley Madison lingered during the 1814 White House fire to rescue it, ordering the canvas removed from its frame and taken away for safe keeping (time did not permit unscrewing the frame from the wall).

Next on the tour is the Green Room, once used as Thomas Jefferson's dining room. Today, it is a first floor parlor and is used for receptions. Most of the furnishings were made by Duncan Phyfe in New York c.1810. The green color scheme began with President Jefferson, who wrote that the room included a "canvas floor cloth, painted Green," and was continued by President and Mrs. James Monroe, who decorated the room with green silks. Under John Quincy Adams, the name "Green Drawing Room" was used , and it has remained the Green Room ever since. The room has been refurbished many times, most recently during the Nixon administration in 1971. Its walls were recovered with delicate watered-silk fabric originally selected by Mrs. John F. Kennedy in 1962, and its draperies are of striped beige, green, and coral silk damask. The carpet is a Turkish Hereke of 19th-century design, and has a multicolored pattern on a green field. A New York sofa table in front of a green, coral, and white striped settee holds a silver Sheffield coffee urn that belonged to John Adams and dates from c. 1785. Presented to the White House in 1964, an engraved, ribbon-hung ellipse above the spigot bears the initials "JAA"-John and Abigail Adams. The urn is flanked by matching silver French candlesticks purchased by James Madison from James Monroe in 1803. Portraits of these two presidents hang over the doors on the west wall here; the Madison portrait is by John Vanderlyn and the Monroe portrait is attributed to Samuel F. B. Morse. Other portraits here include Gilbert Stuarts's portraits of John Quincy and Louisa Catherine Adams, painted in 1818 and 1821, respectively. George Martin's 1767 portrait of Benjamin Franklin hangs over the mantel, an 1858 George P. A. Healy portrait of President James K. Polk, and an 1895 Eastman Johnson portrait of President Benjamin Harrison also hang here.

The next room visitors see is the oval-shaped Blue Room, used by the president to greet guests. Its decor, in French Empire style, was chosen by Monroe in 1817, and was completely renovated under Nixon in 1972. The "blue room" tradition was originated by Martin Van Buren, who redecorated the "oval saloon" in 1837. Today, seven of the French Bellange chairs and one settee selected by Monroe are still in the room. The room also features an early 19th century French Empire gilt wood chandelier encircled by acanthus leaves. The wallpaper frieze, the cornice and the oval plaster ceiling medallion above the chandelier carry out this motif. The draperies, blue satin with handmade fringe and gold satin valances, were copied from an early 19th-century French design. The oval rug, which displays an Oriental adaptation of a French design, was woven in Beijing, c. 1850. On the white marble mantel sits a Hannibal clock, one of the bronze-dore objects purchased for this room by President Monroe in 1817. Portraits hanging in the Blue Room include: an 1819 portrait of Andrew Jackson by John Wesley Jarvis; an 1800 Rembrandt Peale portrait of Thomas Jefferson (painted from life in Philadelphia while Mr. Jefferson was vice president); a 1793 portrait of John Adams by John Trumbull (added to the room in 1986); and an 1859 portrait of John Tyler by George P. A. Healy (considered the finest of a series of presidential portraits painted by Mr. Healy for the White House under a commission from Congress).

The Red Room, the next room on the White House tour, is one of four reception rooms. John Adams used it as a breakfast room, and it was known as the "yellow drawing room" when Dolley Madison used it for her fashionable Wednesday night receptions. Mrs. Madison's portrait, painted by Gilbert Stuart in 1804, hangs in this room today. This was also where Rutherford B. Hayes took the oath of office on March 3, 1877. It was redecorated in 1971 under Nixon, using the American Empire style chosen in 1962 during the Kennedy administration. The furnishings are of the 1810-1830 period, and include a mahogany secretary-bookcase and a mahogany sofa attributed to French-born cabinet maker Charles-Honore Lannuier. Fabrics in the room were woven in the United States using French Empire designs. A neoclassical style white marble bust of Martin Van Buren by Hiram Powers, for which he posed in 1836, is displayed on a wall between the windows. Also in this room is a portrait of Van Buren's daughter-in-law Angelica Singleton Van Buren, who acted as official hostess for the widower president. This portrait was painted by Henry Inman in 1842. On the marble mantel, identical to the one in the Green Room, is a late 18th-century bronze-dore clock given to the White House by French President Vincent Auriol in 1952. The clock plays pastoral music on a miniature organ inside its gilded case. Hanging from the ceiling is a French Empire 36-light chandelier made of carved and gilded wood and dating from about 1805. Albert Bierstadt's *View of the Rocky Mountains*, signed and dated 1870, hangs above an 1825 Empire sofa.

The last room on the tour is the state dining room, with a seating capacity of 140 and is used for state dinners and luncheons. It features English oak paneling dating from the 1902 renovation. The room was enlarged by the McKim firm in 1902. On display during tours here is a long mahogany dining table, surrounded by Queen Anne chairs. On the table are pieces from the gilt service purchased in France in 1817 for President Monroe. Suspended from the ceiling are two rococo revival candelabras from the Hayes administration. The soft green and brown rug was specially woven for this room in 1973 and resembles a 17th century Persian design. Above the mantel is George P. A.

Healy's 1869 portrait of a contemplative President Lincoln, acquired by the president's son, Robert Todd Lincoln. Robert Todd Lincoln's widow bequeathed the portrait to the White House in 1939. Carved into the mantel is the White House motto.

Leaving the White House, visitors walk through the Cross Hall, which extends between the state dining room and the East Room on the state floor. On display in the Cross Hall are marble busts of American diplomat and poet Joel Barlow by Jean-Antoine Houdon and a bust of George Washington after Houdon. A French settee once owned by Monroe is found below Aaron Shikler's 1970 portrait of John Kennedy, and Greta Kempton's portrait of President Harry S. Truman is also on the west end of the Cross Hall. On the east end are other presidential portraits: Lyndon Johnson by Elizabeth Shoumatoff, Richard Nixon by J. Anthony Wills, and Jimmy Carter by Herbert E. Abrams. The presidential seal is displayed above the Cross Hall entrance to the Blue Room.

Passing through the colonnade designed by architect James Hoban, visitors see the North Entrance Hall. Following tradition, portraits of recent presidents hang here and in the Cross Hall. The east and west walls of the North Entrance Hall currently display portraits of Dwight D. Eisenhower and Gerald R. Ford. To the east is the main stairway, along which are portraits of Presidents Wilson, Harding, Franklin Roosevelt and William McKinley. A portrait of Herbert Hoover hangs above an American pier table on the landing. Before state dinners, the president greets guests of honor in the Yellow Oval Room on the third floor, then accompanies them down the main stairway to the East Room where other guests are gathered. The North Entrance Hall is furnished with French Empire gilded furniture used by President Monroe, as well as a French pier table and a pair of French settees with mahogany swan heads purchased by Monroe in 1817.

Many rooms of the White House are used by the president and his family as living quarters or by the president and his staff as offices. These rooms are not included in the tour, and the family dining room, on the state floor, is one such room. On the third floor are: the East Sitting Hall, the Queens' Bedroom (named for its many royal guests), the Lincoln Bedroom, the Lincoln Sitting Room, the Treaty Room (the former Cabinet Room, where President Kennedy signed the Partial Nuclear Test Ban Treaty in 1963), the Center Hall, the Yellow Oval Room, the President's Dining Room, and the West Sitting Hall. The third floor also includes private residential space. The West Wing, where the President and his staff's offices are located, includes: the West Wing Reception Room, the Roosevelt Room (named in honor of Theodore Roosevelt and used for staff meetings and occasional press conferences), the Cabinet Room and the Oval Office.

The White House embodies the rich political, architectural and cultural traditions of the United States. Like the nation whose chief executives resides there, it has evolved and changed over time, and will undoubtedly continue to be redecorated and enhanced to accommodate the changing needs of the president, his family, and the executive branch. With much to learn and see in the most famous house in America, repeated visits to the White House are warranted.

THEODORE ROOSEVELT

Library of Congress

WILLIAM MCKINLEY

Gerald R. Ford Library

GERALD R. FORD

Herbert Hoover Library

HERBERT HOOVER

Ronald Reagan Library

RONALD REAGAN

William Howard Taft NHS

WILLIAM HOWARD TAFT

FRANKLIN D. ROOSEVELT

Franklin D. Roosevelt Library

Adams NHS

JOHN QUINCY ADAMS

GEORGE H.W. BUSH

George Bush Presidential Library

Library of Congress

HARRY S TRUMAN

Clinton Presidential Library

WILLIAM J. CLINTON

Western Reserve
Historical Society

JAMES A. GARFIELD

Bibliography

Clark, Birge M., Memoirs About Mr. and Mrs. Herbert Hoover, With Particular Emphasis on the Planning and Building of Their Home on San Juan Hill, Palo Alto, CA.

Dennis, Ruth, *The Homes of the Hoovers*, Herbert Hoover Presidential Library Association, Inc., West Branch, IA, 1986.

Hamke, Lorethea A., *All About William Henry Harrison*, Frances Vigo Chapter Daughters of the American Revolution, Vincennes, IN, 1985.

Hellman, Susan Holway, "Oak Hill: James Monroe's Loudon Seat," Thesis for the Degree of Master of Architectural History, School of Architecture, University of Virginia.

Kern, Ellyn R., *Where the American Presidents Lived*, Cottontail Publications, Indianapolis, IN, 1982.

Kochmann, Rachel M., *Presidents Birthplaces, Homes, and Burial Sites*, Hass Printing, Park Rapids, MN, 1989.

Krusen, Jessie Ball Thompson, *Tuckahoe Plantation*, Richmond, VA, 1975.

Whitney, David C., *The American Presidents*, Prentice Hall Press, NY, 1990.

About the Authors

Nancy Duffield Myers Benbow is a teacher. She holds a Bachelor of Science degree from Wagner College in New York and a Master of Science degree from the City University of New York.

Christopher H. Benbow is an attorney. He earned a Bachelor of Arts degree from Hampshire College in Massachusetts and holds a Juris Doctor degree from New York Law School.

THOMAS PUBLICATIONS publishes books about the American Colonial era, the Revolutionary War, the Civil War, and other important topics. For a complete list of titles, please visit our website at:

www.thomaspublications.com

Or write to:

THOMAS PUBLICATIONS
P.O. Box 3031
Gettysburg, Pa. 17325